Copyright informal

Foreword

Moira Henderson is a very ordinary Scottish lady. Born in 1960, the youngest of three children and part of a very large extended family. Moira grew up with larger than life characters and a keen sense of right and wrong. Both sides of the family were very caring; a family trait which eventually led to Moira becoming a nurse. This book began as a collection of tales told over the dinner table to various friends and guests. Anecdotes about life on the farm and the challenges she faced with no knowledge of agriculture, provide witty and wise words which can be enjoyed by all ages.

Born and brought up on the West Coast of Scotland, with a heritage of Irish ancestry this story is filled with the unique perspective and humour well known in that area. Set against the backdrop of rural Fife and incorporating journeys across the world including Bolivia in South America there are little nuggets of historical fact from the end of the last century and into the new millennium which will enrich your reading experience.

Moira and her husband David have four children and are grandparents. The family ethos and support has driven this story to print and I'm sure you will be encouraged, enlightened and entertained as you are welcomed to become part of the extended "honorary Henderson" family. As you familiarise yourself with Ring Farm, Misty and the family themselves you'll begin to see the thread of Accessible Tourism as it weaves its way through Moira's life and into the design of The Rings.

Essentially an autobiography, this book tells the story of a journey which came out of a desire to help those who need a holiday; something, which Moira has come to realise, many of us take for granted. Her own family experiences planted the seed of Accessible Tourism and "Inclusion" was in the family before the word had even been coined in society at large. Moira is passionate about improving the Accessible Tourism opportunities in Fife and The Rings project has been identified as a European case study for Accessible Tourism. Working closely with Visit Scotland and the Scottish Government to improve Accessible Tourism she is involved with developing Accessible Tourism Fife, which was launched in November 2015. Moira's combination of dyslexia, determination and faith are enabling people from all backgrounds to visit and stay in a relaxing rural retreat, perfect for making memories like those shared generously in these pages.

The Baroness Grey – Thompson DBL DE

Introduction

On the 13th of August 2014 I made a throw away comment that perhaps I should write a book, not intending for it to be taken seriously. Fergus Ewing MSP said he wanted a signed copy and I laughed. However months later I had been asked several times when would the book be published and I hadn't even started to write it! I knew that if I didn't write this story before we opened The Rings then it wouldn't happen. So, here goes, please be patient with me as I set the scene for why I became so passionate about Accessible Tourism and the building of The Rings in particular. There are a few more "you couldn't make it up" stories in the early years too. Oh, and there are a few funny stories thrown in just for good measure.

I'm dyslexic so it has been a challenge just starting the process of putting words onto paper or the computer screen as it happens. If someone was in the room and I was telling them face to face then I would have no problem, so I have decided just to write this as if we are having a cuppa and I'm telling you the stories as we are relaxing in front of the roaring coal fire in the living room of our farmhouse. The backdrop is the green of what some African friends, who were visiting us, described as the first "natural bush" they had seen since arriving in Scotland. We hope they were describing the fields which can be seen from our living-room window, but worry that they were in fact referring to our garden! The Lomond Hills rise from the horizon and to the left there is a lone tree which punctuates the skyline.

Oh dear, I'm stuck already! Where should I begin? As the song from The Sound of Music goes, "Let's start at the very beginning, a very good place to start".

Chapter 1: Early life

I was a "late baby" born into a family of three children. I have a sister who is eight and a half years older and a brother twelve years older. The age gap meant that growing up was a little bit like being an only child at times. My Dad had been a miner as was his father before him. He had worked on a farm when he left school at first and it made a big impression on him. During the war he was a Fireman on the railways, now this was the man who made the fire in the steam engines and kept it going, not a person who puts out fires, which really confused me as a child. Dad later started his own business, cutting up wood and selling it round the doors. I think there may have been other businesses but when I was born he had lorries which transported farm livestock; from farm to market etc. the experience he had on the farm I'm sure had a hand in this decision. From time to time he would transport other agricultural goods. I remember when I moved to Fife he rhymed off various Farms that he had delivered to and it was only in recent years that I discovered that he would transport other goods for return loads including linoleum from Kirkcaldy, a town still famous for linoleum production.

After the Second World War there was a lack of housing so Mum and Dad's first home when they got married, in June 1945, was a converted railway carriage. I don't think they were unique in their choice of home. My brother was born in my Gran's house but the converted carriage was his home too. Rainwater was collected and used with great care, Mum always said her hair shone because it was washed in rain water. I believe they then progressed to an old cottage, to my knowledge there are no surviving pictures of this house and it was demolished when the new bungalow was built. My siblings say that I was the lucky one as I came along when things were not so financially tough. I was born in the bungalow that my Dad had built in Milton Of Campsie. It was a small country village which nestled itself tightly at the foot of the Campsie Fells, it is probably only about ten miles from Glasgow but for me, at least, it was idyllic.

I still have vivid memories of that house even although I was only six when we left to move to Cambuslang. I loved living in the country and started at the small village school. Mum worked with Dad in his business but I wasn't too aware of this as she was always there in the home.

We went to a small Church in nearby Kirkintilloch, it was called the "Gospel Hall". I was always happy to go as everyone was kind to me. We called the older ladies "auntie" and the men "uncle" it was less formal than Mr and Mrs although the *very old* ladies we called Mrs!

My Dad always had a great care for the widows in the Church and they would often come and stay at our house in Cambuslang for holidays, after we moved there. We also had a "room and kitchen" in Gourock where they went for holidays too. I remember when at school in Cambuslang writing in my "news book" that I was very happy because my Daddy's "lady friends" were coming to stay! I dread to think what the teacher must have thought.

Mrs Lang and Mrs Sneddon came most often and they taught me how to skip. I was hopeless at it and looking back they must have had sore arms "cawing" the rope; they would have been well into their seventies at the time but never complained.

Another fond memory from church at Kirkintilloch was the younger ladies, who would have been teenagers at the time. They would come into the services and a waft of perfume would fill the room, as they walked to their seats their taffeta underskirts made a gentle swishing noise, and the tinkle of their charm bracelets broke the prayerful silence. I'm sure the "Charm bracelets" and their association with "luck" would have been disapproved of in church but to my knowledge it was never said. They were the fashion at the time and to this day I have my little silver charm bracelet in my jewellery box, each trinket still holding a precious memory. These girls were immaculately "turned out" I was in awe of them and thought how wonderful it would be to be like them. The years have taught me that it is not the outward appearance that is important but what is in the heart. Our family has kept in touch with these ladies and they grew into lovely women of God. One sadly was taken still as a young woman after a tragic road accident. I recently met her friend, who was also involved in that accident, at the funeral of her ninety-five year old mother. Another of these teenage girls has become a life-long friend and a very positive role model in my life.

As I said, I had wonderful memories of the bungalow at Milton-of Campsie, the most important would be the night that as I lay in my bed I came to the realisation that I had a black heart and I needed it to be made white! Please don't think I'm going to give you a "Bible-bashing" but it is impossible for me to tell my story without including this vital part. I knew God loved me from what I had gleaned from Sunday school stories and choruses that we sang week by week. One of them sums it up so well:

Jesus loves me this I know,

For the Bible tells me so.

Little ones to Him belong,

We are weak but He is strong.

Yes, Jesus loves me,

Yes, Jesus loves me,

Yes, Jesus loves me,

The Bible tells me so.

The Bible told me that I had sinned, simply explained to me as having a black heart. I knew this even although I was only about five years old. I knew I had done bad things and there was a rebellious side to me. This is a very important point. We tend to categorise sin e.g. murderers, thieves etc. and as a five year old, most would look and say "well she is a good girl". I hadn't really done much wrong but in God's eyes I was still a sinner. Sin separates us from having a relationship with God. The Bible tells us this is why God sent His Son to restore that broken relationship. John chapter 3 verse 16 says it perfectly.

> *"For God so loved the world that He gave His one and only Son that whosoever believes in Him will not perish but have everlasting life."*[1]

That night, as I lay in my bed, I knew I had to ask God to take my sin away, "Make my black heart white and come into my heart to stay". The amazing thing, the miracle is *He did*! And He is still there today. I don't know what the date was but I can remember it as if it was yesterday. That night my name

---

[1] John 3:16 NIV

was written in the Lamb's Book Of Life[2], the date is recorded and one day the book will be opened and my name with the date will be read out. I don't recall the date as I was only a child, so I look forward to knowing it that day, but the important thing is that the Bible tells me that I can only get into heaven if my name is written in that book.

Just a wee thought of another book spoken of in the Bible. It tells us in the Psalms that God has a bottle for our tears and He has recorded them in His book. This is not the Book of Life this is another book, one for our tears. The tears I have shed either for grief or pain, happiness or laughter they are all recorded, that is how interested God is in me and He is just as interested in you. The act of asking God to take your sins away is often called being "Born Again" so interestingly I was born physically and born again, spiritually in that bungalow in Milton of Campsie. That was where my life journey with God began.

Is it in the genes, Lord Sugar?

As I said earlier my Dad had had a livestock haulage business but around the time I was born he sold it and started to make concrete paving slabs and kerb just at the time when building was on the increase and new towns were planned in the 1960s. Although East Kilbride had started in 1947, it continued to grow. Other new towns included Glenrothes in 1948, Cumbernauld in 1956, Livingston in 1962 and Irvine in 1966. Dad supplied the majority of these although Glenrothes was supplied by a local company in Fife. At that

---

[2] Revelation 20:15

time Dad was a member of the Concrete Federation and I remember he spoke of going to the annual dinner. I believe it was a very close community. These towns continued to expand over the following years which contributed greatly to my Dad's expanding business. The new towns were an ambitious solution to build new communities and ease the problems of slum tenements. Other companies such as Wimpy were building and there was a buzzing building and construction industry at that time. These were only two of the different businesses my Dad had in his life.

The factory that made the slabs and kerb was in Cambuslang and we moved there when I was six years old. It was almost an accident that Dad began to manufacture paving slabs. Before the lorries, Dad went into business as an agricultural contractor, spreading lime on fields for farmers and owning a threshing mill which would be towed from farm to farm. The harvest would be cut and fed into the machine which would "thrash" the wheat or barley off the straw, these were the precursors of today's combine harvesters. The company he bought the lime from went into liquidation, so to preserve his supply he bought over the company and with it came a press for making paving slabs. Lime was also used to make lime concrete hence the concrete paving press, so what came as a "by-product" became his main business. It is said Dad's was the first company to have a Hiab crane put on a lorry in Scotland. He took one of his lorries to a company in England, they cut it in half and installed the crane with a "grab" attachment. This meant the slabs could be off loaded at the building sites with ease. Prior to this every very heavy slab had to be man handled off the lorry. This was achieved by sliding them down a plank of wood to the ground then "walking" them to where they needed to be laid. As you can imagine this was very labour intensive and fraught with health and safety issues, although in the sixties this wasn't such a "hot topic".

Dad was quite a sight to behold driving to work in the morning in his Jaguar or Daimler wearing his boiler suit with his bunnet perched at a jaunty angle on his head! Often sales men would call and ask for "Mr Machray" he would tell them to ask at the office. They had no idea they were speaking to the "boss". He drank his tea from a "can" at his work, I think that was a habit from his days on the railway. My sister, who worked in the office would then direct the sales folk to where Dad was drinking his tea, by which time he had disappeared back down to the slab making machine which was called a concrete press.

I worked very briefly for him the summer before I started my nurse training. I was the "mixer" operator. This involved mixing batches of wet gloopy concrete in a large mixer high above the machines. I would access this dizzy height by gingerly climbing up a wooden ladder with my book carefully tucked under my arm. It was all automated and only required pressing buttons in sequence when lights came on to introduce the carefully measured "ingredients". The difficulty came when 2 or more machines had to be "fed". Disaster struck when, I was so busy reading a Nancy Drew mystery that I forgot to move the chute to the next machine resulting in two batches of concrete being put into the one hopper which was not large enough to contain it all. A cascade of concrete poured over my Dad. I will never forget the picture of the concrete dripping off his bunnet on to the end of his nose! Total exasperation written all over his face, the steam puffing out of his ears measured the temperature of his anger. I was rapidly moved to another job, where I couldn't read a book at the same time as I had been doing on the mixer!

I didn't like living in a town and didn't really settle at the school, looking back perhaps it was that I was struggling with my dyslexia/dyscalculia neither of which was recognised in the 1960s. I can well remember being humiliated when I couldn't "recite" my times tables and had difficulty with spelling. I had a wooden duster thrown at me and my fingers rattled with a wooden ruler. It is no surprise that I tried to play "sick" as often as possible. Feeling stupid was my overwhelming memory of that time. I was frustrated as I didn't think I was *stupid*. It has been a relief that in recent years I have been able to understand more about dyslexia and many of my "learning experiences" have been put into context. Much of how I think makes so much more sense now and I can cherish my differences as unique gifts.

In contrast to hating the school I did love the church we attended, Westcoats Evangelical Church. I had lots of friends there of all ages and despite leaving Cambuslang when I was eleven years old I'm still in touch with many of them; the older ones are now in their eighties and nineties.

We moved from Cambuslang to Gourock in 1971 as Dad was going to retire. His love for Gourock grew from staying in our holiday flat right on the main street, known as Kempock Street. To reach the flat you had to pass through a dark "close" into the back of the building and then carefully climb the winding, almost spiral concrete steps, hollowed in the centre after years of footfall. It was known as a "room and kitchen" and had a set in bed, which was a bed "set into" the wall, like in a little alcove. The toilet was on the landing. I don't remember there being a bath and certainly no shower.

There was no central heating either and I think we used electric heaters which sat in front of the empty coal fire, I have no memory of it ever being lit.

Dad's hobby was sailing and he had a cabin cruiser, Vega of Rhu which was moored in the bay, he was a member of the Royal Gourock Yacht Club (RGYC) but we only used it for the benefit of a safe mooring and the little boat which would take us and bags out to our boat. For a short time I was a member of the RGYC sea cadets. I learnt how to tie knots and sail small boats but I didn't have the competitive drive for sailing essential in order to be part of the teams. Socially I never felt that I fitted either. I remember the first evening I went sailing with the cadets, the boat was a "piper" class so a flat deck area with an oblong section cut out. The skipper sat at the helm (rear) and we sat perched along the edge of the oblong hanging on for dear life and jumping back and forward changing ropes as the yacht changed direction. When the yacht keeled over (tipped on its side) you were supposed to put your feet on the other side of the oblong and almost stand up. My problem was that even with my lovely short wellies (designed to be easily kicked off if you fell in the water so you didn't sink with water filled wellies) my wee legs were too short. I managed a few times and then we "came about." I jumped back on the side and promptly started to slide off the boat as if I was on a helter-skelter. Before I knew what was happening I was grabbed by my lifejacket and plonked down beside the helmsman "think you better stay with me" he wasnae a bad looking bloke and I felt safer there than I had all evening, so there was no argument from me.

During the summer months Saturdays would be spent with friends on Vega of Rue sailing "doon the watter" on the

Clyde, a favourite destination being Rothesay on the Isle of Bute. Soup and Auld's pies provided a satisfying lunch then home again in time for a fish supper tea usually with a pickled onion. I loved the boat but Mum hated being on the water unless it was one of the large steamers that filled the Clyde in those days. Sadly only The Waverley, the last ocean paddle steamer, is left as a reminder of the glory days of the Clyde. Thankfully she has been restored and is maintained by a charity. Despite her fear, Mum entertained our guests and tried her best to hide her phobia. She taught me many lessons and this was one of them, to put others first.

When we moved to Gourock I had to repeat primary seven, apparently I was too young to go to the High School. I'm not quite sure how this happened other than perhaps because of the fact that when I started school there were two intakes per year which could have caused the age discrepancy. Gourock Primary seemed different and I had an excellent teacher, Mr Stewart, he had the ability to put many of the "jigsaw pieces" into place and although I still couldn't "do my tables" I seemed to get better results at this school. Was I starting to use "strategies" to get through my difficulties? I wasn't conscious of that but something was better, I went on to high school and with a lot of hard work and other good teachers like Mr Wilson, my maths teacher. I left with eight O-levels and a couple of Highers. Gourock High school only went to 4th year at that time so to sit my highers I had to move to Greenock Academy recently, used for the filming location of the TV series "Waterloo Road".

Another highlight of my High School years were the "Performances" we put on at the end of the year. There were only around 400 pupils in the school. Miss Vitty our only music teacher teamed up with Don McNeil, Principal teacher of Art, Carol Leith, French teacher and Miss Ritchie, Maths, not forgetting Hugh Harris, school technician who was in charge of lighting and sound. We performed Humperdinck's Hansel and Gretel opera and in subsequent years went on to present The Sound Of Music, The King and I and Camelot. Those productions went on to spawn The Oracle Theatre Group which went on for many years and held performances in the Greenock Arts Guild.

During this period Dad had bought a farm on the other side of Glasgow, you thought he was retiring? So did everyone, but he didn't! Interestingly it was a farm above the coal mine he had worked in when a young man. I didn't have any involvement on the farm as I had already started to do my Nurse training at the Argyle and Clyde College of Nursing and Midwifery, in August 1977.

Why did I choose nursing?

The house we lived in at Cambuslang was a large town house that had a "maid's" room, as we didn't have a maid, this is where I played. It was a tiny room off the kitchen backed by the "Esse" solid fuel cooker so it was always snug and cosy. Sometimes I would have it set out as a hospital ward, sometimes as a school room or a café. The school room was a bit odd as I certainly would not have wanted to be a teacher and didn't enjoy school. I would, perhaps have liked to run a café and certainly at times now I feel as if I'm running a restaurant at home but I knew I wanted to be a nurse. My inspiration was my "Ladybird" book on Florence Nightingale. I'm sure I still have it in a cupboard somewhere.

I also had some very positive role models who were nurses including aunts and ladies in the church. So I had no other career ambitions, I would be a nurse and that would be my lifetime career. God had a different plan!

As I said earlier it is impossible to tell this story without speaking about Him. My life as a Christian has had many ups and downs, please don't think that Christians are perfect, they most definitely are not. I can remember though, being challenged as a teenager "if you were taken into a court with the accusation of being a Christian, would there be enough evidence to convict you?" I hope there would be enough evidence against me.

How did I meet my husband?

Gospel Literature Outreach (GLO) was started by an Australian missionary who was concerned about how to reach the world with the good news of the gospel. We have just, in May 2015, celebrated forty years of this outreach mission starting in Motherwell. Part of the work involves teams of young people giving up their holidays and travelling to help missionaries mostly in Europe. My sister went on many of these teams and eventually became a missionary in Italy, she is still there and married to a lovely Italian man.

I decided to go to France for a week on a GLO team in the summer of 1978. I had started my nurse training in August 1977 and as part of the preparation to go to France spent, what was called, an "Orientation" weekend prior to going abroad. This was held at the centre in Motherwell and was to give us an idea of what we would be involved in when we went abroad as well as some guidance on cultural differences etc. It was at this weekend that I met David Henderson, who would become my husband. He was the son of a shepherd and was working on a farm near Edinburgh.

During our nurse training we would spend about four weeks in the college and then we would be let loose on the wards to practise what we had learned in the classroom. After the weekend I met David, we were in college and over coffee the discussion got up about what we had all been doing at the weekend. I announced that I had met this chap whose Dad was a shepherd, he had three older sisters and a twin brother. I nearly fell off the chair when one of the other students, Moira Muirhead, said "are you going with Hugh or David?" She then revealed that her Mum and Dad were very close friends of the Henderson family and there couldn't have been many families who fitted my description. She knew both they and I were Christians so her Sherlock Holmes style announcement was simple deduction. What a small world.

"Courting" as it was then called wasn't easy as David lived on the East coast of Scotland and I on the West, we were two hours apart. I would spend my days off traveling to the East coast and spending time with his Mum or sister during the day and spending time with David in the evenings. On the weekends he would come to Gourock and it was role reversal with David putting up with my family when I was working just to spend a few hours together when I came off duty. David was very useful on the farm Dad had bought near Glasgow, especially as Dad had bought sheep but didn't have much experience with the lambing process. They don't all come on their own and some need the intervention of the shepherd, David was able to pass on the knowledge he had gleaned from his Dad and studied at college. I in turn spent time with his Dad when he was lambing watching him skilfully bring the wee lambs into the world and care for them. At the time I watched with interest but it never occurred to me that I myself would be needing these skills in a few years' time.

Due to the distances we travelled we decided that we would get married when I finished my nurse training. I was only twenty years old and that took a fair bit of convincing and negotiating when David had to ask my Dad for my "hand in marriage". We were married on a scorching hot day on the 27th of September 1980.

As I said when I was going with David he was working on a farm near Edinburgh so I applied to continue my studies at Edinburgh Sick Children's hospital after I completed my general nursing. However David applied and was successful in getting a lecturing job at Elmwood College in Cupar, Fife. It would have been too far for me to travel to Edinburgh to the Sick Kids, and we could only barely afford one car, let alone two. We had managed to get a mortgage and buy a wee house, with a front and back door and a large garden in the village of Windygates. The significance of a back and front door was that house prices in the Greenock area were inflated due to industries like IBM and we probably couldn't have afforded even a small flat had we been staying in my home area. I started working at the Victoria Hospital in Kirkcaldy as a staff nurse on night duty and over the next few years gained experience in Medical, Orthopaedics, Gynaecology and Paediatrics. I took maternity leave to have our daughter Ruth in 1983 and then after Paul came along in

1985 I left the Victoria Hospital and became a "stay at home Mum".

Chapter 2: Starting into Agriculture

The government had introduced Youth Training programmes and these were aimed at giving school leavers skills and the possibility of full time jobs if kept on where they were getting their work experience. The College where David worked were key in the training of these youngsters and one of David's roles was to visit local farmers and liaise with placing students and following their "progress" in their placements. Many of these young teenagers had no interest in Agriculture and even less desire to be at the college. This proved to be a very stressful time for David as often there were frustrations between the employers and employees on the programme. Most people take up golf or some sort of hobby to relieve stress but David started to look into keeping sheep!

Before Ruth was born we moved to Kennoway and had a large garden but not large enough to keep sheep. We found some fields to rent about twelve miles from our home in January 1986 and bought a flock of one hundred and ninety sheep, they were already "in lamb". As it came close to lambing time we bought an old touring caravan and parked it in one of the sheds on the rented farm. We only rented the fields, no house! Just before the lambing started we "moved" into the caravan, Ruth was three and a half and Paul about seven months old. Those were the days of "terry nappies", disposables were just coming out but they weren't very good and you had more washing of clothes due to leaks than nappies to wash!

We moved in on the Friday after David finished at the college for the weekend, the crash course began in sincerity on the Saturday morning. David walked me around the sheep, instructing me as we went about what to do if this or that was happening. This was repeated on the Sunday.

It's a fank-less task!

The weekend drew to a close and David went off to college on the Monday morning. The children and I had an uneventful morning, which I now realise was the calm before the storm, all would change in the afternoon.

I don't think I'm exaggerating when I say Mirk, our sheep dog, knew more about lambing than I did. As I took a "reckie" around the field to see if any action was about to happen I spotted a ewe trying to deliver a lamb. The head was out but no sign of any legs. I knew that there had to be at least one leg popping out or the ewe wouldn't be able to get the body of the lamb through her pelvis. When you are a nurse on most occasions your patient is waiting patiently for you in the bed, when you are a shepherd you have to catch the brute first. I parked Ruth out of harm's way beside a bale of straw and started charging after a ewe which I could see was needing assistance, with Paul on my back in a baby carrier. I'm not quite sure what I thought I could do when, or even if, I caught the ewe with Paul on my back, but I quickly realised that this wasn't working. These were the days before mobile phones, so there was no SOS call to David at work, nor was there the opportunity to "phone a friend" for advice.

I sat there, the sun beating down making it unusually hot for a spring day, tears of frustration and exhaustion ran down my face while beads of perspiration trickled down my back and the backs of my legs. My feet were throbbing with the heat and exertion, not helped by the thick woollen socks now soaking up the evidence of my exertion.

Too many layers on for the task in hand I now realised wasn't the best decision. That wasn't the only decision I had got wrong. To rent some farm land and buy a couple of hundred ewes, in lamb, didn't seem so crazy, more like an adventure. It had seemed a good idea at the time and since then many have asked why we did it? Sitting in that field with no one to help I was wondering the same thing; the spirit of adventure was diminishing. Watching programmes now like "Escape to the Country" I hear these unsuspecting townies say "I just want some sheep, hens and a goat, oh and some alpacas would be good." Are they mad? No, they just haven't a clue how hard it is to care for livestock, especially when you don't know what you are doing.

A little hand patted my arm "It's okay Mummy, don't cry, Daddy will know what to do," Ruth was trying to bring some rationale and reassurance into the situation. By now the ewes were starting to settle back to munching at the grass after their umpteenth chase around the field. I often wonder what they must have thought, the score was totting up and they were definitely winning. Their main focus now was "food" to replenish lost calories from their unplanned fitness challenge.

Mirk our well-trained collie had also stepped down into "stand-by" mode looking at me expectantly knowing that the job wasn't finished, awaiting his next command. In my brief training period, I had also had to learn a set of commands that the dog would understand, "That'll do" should bring the dog to heel. "Come-by" sends the dog in a clockwise direction and "way to me" should send the dog anti-clockwise around the sheep. The final command being "walk on" if you wanted the dog to move forward.

Then a kick in the back brought me back to reality with a jolt. Paul, perched in a baby carrier on my back, clearly had not grasped the seriousness of the situation. He kicked as a rider would kick to encourage the horse to move on, giggling at the fun he'd had and the prospect of more, he wanted it now. Realising that it would be impossible to catch the ewe with Paul on my back I then hung him in his carrier on a fence post and set off again. Mirk was running back and forward looking expectantly at me, waiting for commands which I never gave. I could remember the commands but in the stress of the situation couldn't remember which went with the action I needed the dog to take.

I had tried to listen to all the instructions given from David. I supplemented this with my nurse training, the most relevant bit being four weeks obstetric nursing. I racked my brains trying to recall what I'd seen when casually watching what my father-in-law did when I would visit during the lambing. But now I was "in at the deep end" and most, if not all the instructions had fled in the panic, it felt like they were running ahead of the sheep I was trying to catch.

For many reading this it will be difficult for you to imagine a day without mobile phones or Google but I didn't have any of these "helps" we take so much for granted today. To prove the point I have just googled "how to catch a sheep" and I have videos, text and plenty of them to choose from. I didn't have these luxuries back in 1986, nor could I phone David at the college to ask where I was going wrong, the nearest phone box was three miles away and he wasn't often in his office.

I had to try again, so I sat Ruth on the straw bales that were positioned in the corner of the field, near where Paul still hung on a fence post and set off with Mirk, the most intelligent and qualified member of the team. He did his best to keep the flock together but it was clear he was unsure as to what I was playing at because I still couldn't get the commands right.

After about two hours of these antics, I had had enough so had the ewes, in hind sight it was a miracle that they didn't all start lambing that afternoon. I put Paul back on my back and wearily led Ruth back to the shed. Paul began to nod off in his baby carrier; the fresh air and excitement causing him to drift into a sleepy state.

The dated touring caravan was a welcome place of refuge. Yes, you are right I do have a screw missing. Who in their right mind would stay in a touring caravan in a dark shed for weeks in the chilly months between winter and spring to do smelly dirty work with a three year old and seven month old?

I was angry. Angry at the ewe for being so stupid not to let me help her. Angry that I couldn't catch her, knowing there was something I had missed but couldn't think what it was. Angry at David for not being there and angry at myself for getting myself into this situation. So I did what we Brits do best and had a cup of tea. Oh that was of course, after I had helped my infant jockey dismount, and settled him for a nap in the bunk. I pulled off our wellies and stripped Ruth and me of several layers of waterproofs, jackets and jumpers.

David eventually came home from the college and as I poured out my frustration and concerns about the ewe and not being able to help her, he looked at me with a quizzical look and said,

"Why didn't you use the fank?"

"What is a fank?" I retorted.

"Everyone knows what a fank is," he replied.

"I assure you, not everyone knows what a fank is!" I shouted with exasperation.

None of this conversation was sorting out the problem of the ewe with the "head only" lamb. We pulled all our gear on and Paul stirred from his nap, excited at the prospect of "Rodeo – The Sequel". We made our way back to the lambing field.

Now do you remember me saying I had settled Ruth by the bales of straw in the corner of the field? Well I was to be enlightened that these bales of straw were said "fank"! The idea is that the straw bales are positioned to make an enclosure with a gate at one end, into which expert working dog, Mirk, would assist me by rounding up the sheep. He would walk forward pushing them into the enclosure with me quickly closing the gate behind them. The result is all the sheep are close together making it impossible for them to run away, so the shepherd (me) can work their way to the target ewe to be assisted. Now this still can't be done with rodeo boy, Paul on back, the solution is to hang carrier and boy on a fence post enabling shepherd to complete the task without killing herself and the children. It was so obvious, but then things always are "once you know how"!

We were Baa-rmy!

The following day was much better and with the great assistance of "Mirk" we had a more positive outcome. Having small hands I became quite good at reaching places inaccessible to others with larger hands, use your imagination, I don't want to be too graphic!

Every night we would gather the ewes into the shed where they waded through the freshly prepared straw, they would settle then get onto their feet and move around, giving each other a wee shove fighting over a particular "patch" which to the human eye looked pretty much the same as the next bit. Whether there was any difference or if this was a game like sheep snakes and ladders, I don't know, but it was quite amusing to watch.

Typical of a four-berth touring caravan the dining table had to be lowered and slotted into position before pulling the cushions down to make the mattress. Then you can make the bed. You can imagine with clothes, toys and sheep necessities, there wasn't much room and I found myself doing a constant dance of shuffling "stuff". It wasn't easy getting the children to sleep and then manoeuvring past them to get to the door for the hourly checks on the expectant mothers.

I would check the ewes until about 2am then David would get up at about 5am so there was only a three hour slot that wasn't covered. We would put out the lights and surprisingly few would lamb during these hours. Sometimes when I was feeling particularly exhausted I would just have a wee "keek" through the curtains. It was quite surreal, lying in bed looking out to a sea of woolly, rotund mums-to-be, listening for the strange little noises that a ewe makes when in the latter stages of labour. There can be a great deal of scraping of the straw with a hoof. As if fluffing it up to make it more comfortable or it may look like she is trying to uncover a buried lamb, "sorry pet you have to do the work, they don't just appear from under the straw," I would think to myself. Sometimes you would hear a grunting from a ewe followed by a little bleat the sound only made by a new born lamb.

Like humans it is better for the ewe if she can be left to lamb herself without intervention but in those early days I had other time factors to fit in such as meals, so sometimes I was tempted to intervene which usually backfired and would end up taking longer.

I soon got into the swing of things and after mastering the use of the "fank". I became more able to catch the ewe in the squeeze of the rest of the flock. I was never too fussed as to how I wrestled them to the ground. The proper way is to catch them with one hand under their chin and turn their head to face towards their back at the same time pushing them down with the other hand. Now, not being too tall (all of five foot nothing) and my arms being in proportion to my height this often resulted in a situation where the ewe was larger than I could even reach round. This then involved using whatever tactic could be mustered to tip the ewe over on her side. The primary aim being to get and keep all four of the ewe's feet off the ground. I quickly learned that any slight connection of hoof to terra firma would result in the ewe springing to her feet and the process would have to start all over again. Second time around there was the disadvantage of the ewe realising what you were trying to achieve.

I remember an occasion, several lambing times later, when we had moved to Ring Farm. It was about 2am and I had already spent about an hour trying to catch this ewe in the shed. We were no longer in a caravan but at least could return to the comfort of our farmhouse with the luxury of a shower, washing machine and our own beds. I had mounted the ewe's back and was being carried around the shed like a rodeo cowboy. I did manage to get one hand under her chin but there I was stuck. The other ewes tried to clear a path for these two wrestling women and to this day, I'm not sure what happened next, but there was a definite role reversal. I found myself lying flat on my back with a weighty woolly warrior lying on top of me. I had successfully got all four hooves off the ground but was in no position to lamb her! As we both lay there heaving, I found my face buried in her warm slightly damp wool coat. Her wool gave off a pungent aroma; the smell of the lanolin which I could feel rubbing off onto my hair. The other ewes in the shed, started to come closer to investigate proceedings, their inquisitive natures getting the better of them. The clean straw moulded its way around my body and I momentarily though, "this must have been what a straw mattress felt like," it was quite jaggy! There was no getting a positive from this position so reluctantly I let the ewe go and started all over again. Use the fank I hear you say. But inside the shed there was no fank. There was, however, a pile of gates ready to build a moveable fank, but tired from looking after three children and by this time a pile of hens, I hadn't the strength to lift and position the gates.

However, I digress, back to Canty Hall, where we were renting fields. After two years we realised we had a serious problem. Our lambs didn't thrive after they were weaned from their mothers. Initially the vet said we had a worm problem so the next year we wormed them religiously, they still failed. David felt it was something called "Pine" which describes how the lambs were "Pining away". This disease is only found on selenium deficient soil and initially David was told there was no such soil in Fife, this is why the vet hadn't thought this to be the diagnosis. However we later found that the three fields we were renting were the only selenium deficient fields in Fife! It was frustrating as we could have bought wormer with added selenium. By this time we had lost a fair bit of money as our crops of lambs had not produced as much income as we would have expected. Our accountant advised that perhaps we should call it a day. I wasn't fighting that advice as it had been hard going spending about 9 weeks of the year in a small, sometimes cold, caravan with two small children often having to share with lambs which were needing "intensive care".

Prior to renting the fields we had thought about trying to buy a farm and had looked at quite a few, mostly in the central belt and the West of Scotland, this would have involved David giving up his lecturing and going full time into agriculture. Thankfully the bank would not support us in this and all the costings, business plans and budgeting fell on deaf ears.

"For I know the plans I have for you."[3]

A short time later our accountant phoned and told us of Ring Farm. It was only ninety acres but being close to Cupar meant that David could still work at the college to give financial security. We could rent out some of the ground to start with and then gradually work our way back into having a flock of sheep again. I didn't mind this as we would at least have a house. We had earlier put our house in Kennoway on the market, having moved from Windygates to Kennoway before Ruth was born.

Our house had been on the market for months with no interest when we realised that the company selling it had taken pictures of the much smaller janitor's house. Ours had previously been the headmaster's house for the nearby primary school and was much larger than the janitor's house. People looking at the picture would immediately have decided that the asking price was too high.

We moved to another selling agent and after much prayer put in an offer for Ring Farm, it was substantially lower than the asking price and it came as a surprise when we got a phone call asking if we could consider raising the offer slightly. We agreed but asked that the entry date be delayed by six months to allow us time to sell our Kennoway home. This was accepted and we started to make plans. We had sold most of our flock to give us the deposit for the farm. The owner of Ring Farm was a Mr Macrae which was a bit of a coincidence as my maiden name was Machray. He, very

---

[3] Jeremiah 29:11 NIV

kindly, allowed us to move our few sheep to Ring Farm before we had formally bought the farm.

The days and weeks went past with still no interest in our house, we started to get concerned, it had been on the market for over one year by this time and we only had one viewing! We were coming very close to the end of the six month "grace" period and the farm would have to be paid for soon. David had an appointment with the bank manager one Thursday evening after work, we knew that the bank would insist on us putting the farm back on the market as without the sale of our Kennoway house we could not pay for the farm and couldn't have two mortgages.

Having two small children and trying to keep your house tidy for viewings had become very trying especially when no one seemed to want to come and view. The house was in a guddle the Wednesday morning prior to David's appointment at the bank the next day.

My doorbell rang.

I went to the door and a young woman of slight build and fair hair announced that she was there to buy our house. In shock I asked would she not like to come in and see what she was going to buy, all the while my mind was racing to images of unmade beds, towels strewn in the bathroom, dirty dishes and a pile of ironing. Thankfully she declined my invitation but requested she return that afternoon with her husband and Mum who stayed with them. She added they had dogs and wanted the house because of the large garden and the fact we had no immediate neighbours which the dogs could disturb. We had playing fields on three sides and the fourth side was the boundary wall of the cemetery[4].

I closed the door and started a major clear up, the difficulty, as anyone who has been in the position of selling a house will know is you can't just "hide" items in cupboards as the prospective buyer usually wants to see every nook and cranny. I don't know who was more excited at the prospect of someone coming to look at the house, me or the prospective buyers. There was no need for a "hard sell" as they had pretty much made up their mind they were buying. Remember these were the days before mobile phones so I hadn't been able to contact David and tell him what had happened. He arrived home from the college to a squad of folk coming out of our large double garage at the end of their tour. "This is the family who are going to buy the house," I explained. His bottom jaw hit the floor before he quickly recovered.

It was with much relief that David announced to a rather puffed up bank manager that we had indeed managed to sell our Kennoway house. The old man had the wind taken out of his sails but recovered sufficiently to grunt an "oh well that's that then"! There was a problem in that the couple had requested a five month delay in taking the keys to give them a chance to sell their property. This would involve us going onto a bank "bridging loan" not the best situation to be in especially with interest rates about 15% which meant we were paying about 18% on the bridging loan for the full amount of the farm. Here we were in 1987 with one wage, our house mortgage and a bridging loan to pay which amounted to more than the monthly wage David was earning. Clearly the figures didn't balance. We prayed. I

---

[4] I have vivid memories of standing at my upper hall window looking over to the cemetery, watching the funeral with full military honours of Captain David Alexander Wood, killed in action 28th May 1982 aged 29, in the Falkland Islands.

---

must admit I had a bit of an argument with God along the lines of, "You clearly wanted us to have the farm or we wouldn't have got it, why are You letting all this extra money go to the bank, is that not a waste?"

God's ways are not our ways and as the months went past we were amazed that every month we had just the right amount of extra money to pay the bridging loan. It came in different ways, a friend told me of a nursing home only about half an hour away, looking for night staff and I was taken onto the team. The shift started at 10pm so it didn't interfere with any services at our church. We were small in number and I was conscious of my responsibility to attend as often as possible. I was able to come off duty and dash home before David had to leave to go to the college so we didn't have any child care costs. We received an unexpected tax rebate too. It was sheep shearing time and David was heavily involved in that at weekends, evenings and when the college closed for the summer holidays. I have no doubt that the lesson we were learning was that it was God who was taking us to Ring Farm and it would be by His provision alone that we would remain there.

Ring Farm - "we are here now" (as our satellite navigation system would say with a French accent.)

The house at Ring Farm hadn't been lived in for about fifteen years and needed re-wired, plastered, central heating, a new bathroom and there was no kitchen, only a sink. We moved in the month of July 1988, it was freezing, only managing to get two rooms just about habitable before we moved. Our kitchen cupboards, which had been kindly built up by a friend, were all sitting in the middle of the living room floor resulting in a maze-like walk to get through to the rooms we could live in. We only had running water in the bathroom so dishes were washed in the small bathroom sink. I should add that baby number three was on the way at this time.

The day after we moved, some of the few sheep we had left were ready for the market, so to escape what were quite dire living conditions I decided we would all go to the market in Cupar. I said it was cold, the house needed dried out not having been occupied for so many years, so as the heating wasn't fully installed and working we had two coal fires and kept them stoked up. We had got dressed and had breakfast in front of one of the fires and left all the dishes and PJ's lying. When we came back from the market a car followed us down the farm road, to my horror it was my "new" health visitor. I guided her past the kitchen units, which were still sitting in the middle of the living room floor waiting to be fitted into the kitchen, and into our make shift living room. I hastily cleared the PJ's and chucked them behind the settee whilst throwing something over the dishes to hide them in a vain attempt to cover our primitive living conditions. I was still working night shift at the nursing home two nights a week and had two under-fives. This professional lady proceeded to lecture me on the importance of getting enough rest and not pushing myself too much. I was glad to see the back of her and my conclusion was she was totally mad and divorced from reality. How could I sit and rest when living in a partial building site and a new baby due to arrive in six months' time?

After a lot of hard work we settled in to our new home. Ruth started at Craigrothie Primary School in primary one and loved it. Paul was at the playgroup in Ceres and at times would rather have stayed with me at the farm! Jonathan arrived in a bit of a hurry at Ninewells hospital in Dundee on the 11th of January 1989, so he is our only Dundonian. He was the first baby born at Ring Farm in living memory or so we were told by our neighbours. Six weeks later we were lambing.

It wasn't easy with three children under the age of six, the youngest being breast fed. It was a constant round of school and playgroup run, then back to give Jonny a feed and settle him. With the baby monitor attached to my belt I'd don my wellies and head for the lambing shed. Back in before dashing to playgroup, I'd feed the boys again then head out to the shed with Paul in tow. Back in to top up Jonny... etc etc. Some weeks later I was running out of steam and patience, I couldn't satisfy Jonny and decided to give him a bottle to "top him up". I thought I had better touch base with the health visitor and ask advice on any preferred formula. I had a couple of samples from my "bounty bag" which I had received from the hospital. My health visitor was out on visits and a very well-meaning lady answered my call. She encouraged me to rest, eat well and feed on demand. I'm not sure how I managed, but as controlled as I could be in the situation I informed the voice on the other end of the phone that I had two other children and I was lambing one hundred and twenty ewes (our flock had grown again) and if she didn't tell me what to give my baby I would take him outside and stick him under an old ewe to suckle because I was fed up with him sooking *me*! The wise woman backtracked and encouraged me to, "give him whatever you have in the house!" I dutifully made up a bottle which he spat and spluttered and pushed out with his wee tongue firmly holding his lips together to prevent this offending material entering his mouth again. Arghhhhh! Not one to lose a battle easily I thought of my Gran Miller's advice and quartered a tea biscuit, soaked it with some cooled boiled water and mixed it into a paste. The teaspoon only touched Jonny's lips when the mouth was opened and the delights of a tea biscuit were quickly devoured, a change of nappy, a burp and a wee comforting drink sent him off into a relaxed and more prolonged sleep allowing me to attend to my other chores.

Chapter 3: The Hen and Egg years!

Just a little gift

After a few years David came home from the college with a gift for me. Now, most women receive flowers from their husbands and I'm sure in hindsight David wishes he had brought flowers home that day, but instead I received 6 bantam hens. The college had a small animals unit and they had been hatched out for the students but they had no room to keep them so they were given a home at Ring Farm. I loved the wee eggs these dainty ladies laid although finding them was often an adventure in itself. They had a great ability to hide them and as they had complete freedom of the steading, there were plenty of hiding places. One hen had disappeared and we thought she had come to some sad end, when one day David moved a bale of straw and her hiding place was revealed. There she was, sat perched on top of a mound of little eggs, carefully placed like a Ferrero Rocher chocolate pyramid.

Sadly after a weekend visiting my parents in Gourock we returned and the fox had taken all my little ladies. I decided that I had enjoyed the bantams and eggs and that we would replace them with proper sized hens. Now this was at the time of the Mrs Edwina Currie debacle when there was a nationwide scare over salmonella in eggs. If you haven't realised by this stage of the story, that I had a screw missing, then you will now. I thought I could buy some extra hens and sell the spare eggs to friends or perhaps there would be a bigger market out there.

To sell eggs on, you had to test them for salmonella by taking what is called a Cloacal swab. These swabs had to be paid for in batches of twenty-five. Being a true Scot and wanting value for money I thought it sensible to keep twemty-five hens so I could say that "All our hens are Salmonella tested". When I was thinking of my market, I asked myself who would be interested in knowing all the hens were tested? The answer was there from my nursing background, Nursing Homes would want safe eggs! So I started to phone local nursing homes to see if I could supply them with my straight from the farm, very fresh eggs. One responded positively but I nearly collapsed when they said they would take fifteen dozen every week! I only had twenty-five hens at that point and they would only supply about ten dozen per week when they were on full lay. As a rule of thumb one hen will lay an egg for six days then have a day of rest. I've always liked that analogy, if it sounds familiar to you it's because the Bible teaches that God created the world in seven days, the last of which was a day of rest.

I, like most of us, hadn't really thought a great deal about eggs. I knew they generally came from hens and you bought a pack of six, twelve, fifteen or eighteen at the supermarket. I had no idea of the number of eggs consumed daily in the UK or how many hens needed to be kept to produce these eggs. It was a revelation to me that there were many substantial industries supporting the production of eggs. Firstly there are the breeders and believe it or not the "parent" stock can be worth a small fortune as there have been many years of selective breeding to produce the most productive hens who can maintain good sizes and produce for a reasonable period of time before becoming non-profitable. Secondly, there are the farms who rear the young birds. They care for the day old chicks after hatching to the point just before they start to lay. Thirdly, the feed producers; there is a whole science behind getting the poultry food at just the right balance to ensure that they have the right nutrition to stay healthy and reduce the risk of osteoporosis, which leads to bone fractures. The food needs to be consistent. Hens are very fickle wee ladies, any change and they get stressed and either reduce their productivity or down tools all together and you have no eggs to sell. They probably have a more balanced diet than you or I. Fourthly, there is an industry that supplies the packaging whether it be fibre (cardboard) or plastic. There are trays, pre-packs (which Joe Bloggs would call egg boxes) larger cardboard outer boxes (egg farmers call these egg boxes, just to confuse matters), tape to seal the boxes, labels, this list goes on.

In the UK the industry is highly regulated with government inspectors and regulatory bodies which you can "sign up to". One such body is The British Egg Industry Council (BEIC) which was the successor to the old "Egg Marketing Board". You may know of their brand "The Lion Code", there are also associations such as The Red Tractor and Freedom Foods.

Anyway, back to my hens, twenty-five quickly expanded to fifty. Remember the batches of twenty-five swabs. Not long after we started to supply the nursing home, the village shop owner called me up and asked me to start supplying them too. More hens had to be bought and then I was told that I had to register and "grade" my eggs. I was now under the jurisdiction of an Egg Inspector, a lovely and very supportive man, Bill Sinclair, who ensured I did things legally. He also knew I had no background and was willing to teach and encourage me.

Grading my eggs involved a set of digital kitchen scales and a rubber band! Each egg was placed in the rubber band, an ingenious invention of mine, designed to prevent rolling and breaking. The egg was weighed and placed in the appropriate weight group. When I first started keeping hens, we had 7 grades but soon due to EU regulations the grades were narrowed down to Extra Large, Large, Medium and Small. When my flock had grown to 300 hens this method of grading was quite laborious and time consuming. Grading was not the only requirement, they had also to be "candled", which involved a specialist bright lamp. You held the egg against the lamp and rolled it to look for any external imperfections such as cracks in the shell. Any imperfections internally would also be noticeable, such as blood or meat spots, which are bits that "break off" the internal parts of the hen and become "incorporated" into the egg. The air sack also is examined which indicates how fresh the egg is. Housewives in the past would test the freshness of eggs by placing them in a bowl of water. A fresh egg will sink to the bottom and possibly lie flat on the bottom. However if the egg was buoyant with the point facing down to the bottom of the dish this would indicate that it is old, the reason being that as the egg deteriorates the air sack (at the blunt end) fills up with gas from the deterioration process making the egg float in water. How it's made

Have you ever stopped to think of the miracle of how the hen produces an egg? I certainly hadn't but it is wonderful! I never tire of telling the story. The start of the process is ovulation, which is similar to humans in that the ovum (yolk) matures and is released into a funnel of the egg-making "tube". It is sucked in, a bit like a vacuum hoover due to the peristaltic process of the tube as the eggs progress through at different stages of development. Peristalsis is the same action a human body has when you take food in at one end and it emerges at the other in the form of ...sorry, am I giving you too much detail? The white of the egg is added and has to be the right consistency, like a semi-set jelly, for the shell to be added smoothly.

When I was younger my Gran Miller, who lived until she was ninety-six, bought her wool in "hanks" the process of rolling it into balls had to be done before the knitting could begin. I would sit at her feet with my arms outstretched holding the "hank" while Gran unwound the wool and rolled it into a ball. This is how the hen lays down the calcium which becomes the shell, like winding a ball of wool. However here is the bit you couldn't make up, within this process there are about thirty thousand "pores" incorporated. If the egg is fertilised then a chick will grow, it will feed off the yolk but it also needs oxygen until it hatches, human babies get this through the placenta, the chick gets it through the pores, a true miracle. It is through these pores that bacteria can enter the egg but there are significant safety measures which have been designed to protect the chick. The first layer of defence is the "cuticle". When the egg is laid it is wet but it is hot from coming out of the warm body of the hen. It quickly dries out, this creates a protective barrier which, if complete, is very effective. The second defence is the shell itself. If you have boiled and shelled an egg you will be aware of the paper layer which lies between the shell and the white, or albumin, of the egg. There are in fact two layers but this is seldom obvious to the eye, this is also a defence against bacteria. The white of the egg itself is a third and final defence, it contains natural antibiotic properties which will fight for twenty-eight days against any bacteria which makes it through the outer defences, in an attempt to prevent it reaching the nutritious yolk and potentially growing chick. If the bacteria reaches the yolk it has everything it needs to multiply quickly. Another "you couldn't make it up" fact. This is why we have "Best Before" dates of twenty-eight days from point of lay.

When I was nursing we always had eggs on the ward, this was in the late seventies, remember. Eggs were ideal for preparing a quick nutritious meal if someone was admitted but had missed a meal time or if someone didn't feel like eating the food offered on the menu. A little scrambled egg or even a "switched egg" could be made if they had no appetite. The latter would horrify people today due to the concept of eggs being considered "high risk" for salmonella, we will return to that later. For those reading this who don't know what a "switched egg" is, let me enlighten you:

First, separate the white from the yolk.

Whip up the white as you would for a meringue.

ADD SOME SUGAR AND WHIP AGAIN.

CAREFULLY FOLD IN THE YOLK AND ADD SOME MILK GENTLY.

A LITTLE BRANDY OR SHERRY FOR MEDICINAL PURPOSES CAN ALSO BE ADDED.

Knowledge of an "invalid diet" and "switched egg" were an essential part of a nurse's training. After all, if the body doesn't receive the necessary building blocks found in a nutritious diet, how will it repair itself when illness strikes? Oral hygiene was also vital, a furred tongue will inhibit taste and that is important in encouraging an appetite. Ill-fitting dentures or painful teeth make eating certain foods impossible and so a soft diet may be necessary until treatment or better fitting dentures can be arranged. That is just a wee "taster" of Basic Nursing Care.

We also used eggs for wounds. The white of the egg was whipped up again as you would for meringues. It would then be lightly applied to pressure (bed) sores or leg ulcers. It was years later when I attended Glasgow University for the day and Professor Sally Solomon told me of the natural antibacterial in the white of the egg that I made the connection with the wound dressings I had used in my nursing days. By whipping the white we were incorporating oxygen making it hard for anaerobic bacteria to survive and the antibacterial properties of the egg white must have killed some of the bacteria. When it dried it produced something akin to an artificial skin. The Professor confirmed that these were legitimate factors and so it wasn't just an "old wife's remedy".

Eggs, they're the business!

Sorry, that was a bit of a tangent, back to the story. Through word of mouth (I didn't know about marketing or advertising) more customers came along and my flock had to grow. Bit by bit, we added to the flock until we had about three hundred hens. Grading the eggs on a set of kitchen digital scales was laborious and time consuming, so I asked Bill (my Egg Inspector) if he could look out for a table top egg grading machine which would be much quicker. He then informed me of a local producer who was wanting to retire. He had a grading machine for sale and encouraged me to go and chat to him. In due course Ian McIsaac was contacted and I arranged a suitable time to view the grading machine.

When I viewed it I couldn't believe the size of it, "Table-top" it most definitely was not! It stood alone in its own building and was about thirty-five feet by fifty feet. One end had a vacuum attachment which lifted thirty eggs off the tray and gently placed them on a roller conveyor. This was slightly familiar to me as the machine Dad had for making paving slabs had a similar vacuum to lift the slab out of the mould and place it on a pallet to dry. The eggs then were rolled back and forwards over the candling unit which was enclosed by a curtain to darken the area and help to show imperfections. From there they dropped gently onto the weighing part. This was a long shaft that moved back and forward and lifted the eggs weighing them as it did so, if the egg was the right weight a little plastic finger pushed it off and the egg rolled down the lane (similar to a bowling lane only smaller). At the other end of the lane stood the person who was going to pack them into whatever packaging was appropriate, sometimes trays or pre-packs, which would be the packaging many would be most familiar with. The egg would be lifted and weighed, lifted and weighed until it arrived at its appropriate lane be it Extra Large (XL) Large (L) , Medium (M) or Small (S).

I quickly informed Mr McIsaac that there had been some mistake and I had no need of a grader that size. He said that I would need it if I were to take on the cages too. This was news to me, at no point was it ever mentioned that I would be taking on cages! I had to this point been totally convinced that Free Range was the only "proper" way to keep hens. I strongly advised the seller that I totally disagreed with cages and thought it cruel to keep them in this way. He asked if I had ever seen hens in cages and I had to reply that I had only seen pictures on the television. He asked if I would come and listen at the door of the shed, I would not have to go in unless I wanted to.

As I stood at the closed door and listened to the birds gently crooning and clucking away, I was quite surprised. They sounded just the same as my free range hens did. Now, I should add for those who are not familiar with hens, if a hen isn't happy, I can assure you that you can tell very quickly by the noises it makes. Almost before I realised, I was in the shed to look at the hens. There was only a very slight "animal" smell mixed with the appetising smell of hen feed. The birds were well feathered and tucking into lovely clean feed in front of them. They had fresh water supplied and accessed by tapping a "nipple drinker" with their beak. The eggs which had been laid had gently rolled, spotlessly clean onto a conveyor belt. Ian went on to show me how the dung (hen pen) fell through the floor of the cage and onto another conveyor belt which took it cleanly out of the shed on a daily basis. I couldn't believe how clean it all was and how happy and content the birds obviously were. My preconceptions and misconceptions were certainly turned on their head that day.

Sally Solomon did a fascinating study on the welfare of hens. She was a researcher in Glasgow's School of Veterinary Medicine. They were investigating how to help protect endangered species of birds. Shell quality is critical in the viability of the chick. To assist with this research they first looked at the domestic laying birds and factors affecting shell quality. The outcome of the research showed that the least stressed hens were those kept in conventional cages. The most stressed were those in the Free Range units.

With three hundred hens I was becoming aware of the difficulties of keeping larger numbers of hens together. The well-known phrase "The Pecking Order" is related to birds. Hens definitely have a "pecking order". Bright sunny days could trigger the pineal gland and hens predisposed to cannibalism would go on to attack their neighbours. Then there were predators, in the form of foxes, badgers or hawks, hens are easy targets. Furthermore, keeping the eggs clean in my free range system was a nightmare. If you wash them they are no longer "class A" so can't be sold for human consumption.

I became a little like the man on the Remington shaver advert who said, "I liked the shaver so much I bought the company". I took advice from friends and family who kept hens and had sold eggs. They said if the business came with a delivery route and customer base it would be worth having. After some research and a trip to the bank manager, we took the bold step of not only buying the grading machine but purchasing the business. This involved building a new shed to house the grading machine and packaging material which was then called "The Packing Shed". We dismantled the hen sheds at one farm and transported them the four miles to Ring Farm to be re-erected. This had to be done over a considerable period of time. We had to keep the supply of eggs going so as one flock was coming to the end of the lay and the shed was emptied, the whole shed was taken to bits. The pieces were numbered and the parts were loaded onto trailers and moved to Ring Farm where the building process would begin, a bit like a giant Lego model.

As part of the agreement Ian would train me in poultry keeping, known as "Poultry Husbandry". The business included marketing under the brand name used by Ian "Best out of Fife" as well as the customer base of hotels, guest houses, Bed and Breakfast accommodation, shops, and St Andrews University, although this was a customer I would have to tender for annually. Ian would also direct and assist in the dismantling and re-erection of the hen sheds and we would provide someone to assist and help with the physical work. He was getting on in years and not in the best of health, hence his reason for retiring. Little did we know how little time he had left this side of eternity. He had passed on a significant amount of information to me but his illness, which we knew nothing of during the discussions, overcame him quickly and he was admitted to hospital with terminal bone cancer. David visited him in hospital and asked him was he prepared. He told David that his burial plot was paid for and his affairs were in order. David encouraged him to think about what would happen after he died but Ian didn't enter into any discussion and drifted off to sleep, that was the last conversation David would have with him.

I can remember when Ian was training me, he knew we were Christians and said, "You will have to forget about church. Your business has to come first". I had learned a little chorus when at Sunday school at Westcoats in Cambuslang, it went like this:

Store your treasure in the bank of heaven,

Where no thief can steal it away,

There you'll find it safely waiting for you,

When you get to heaven, one day.[5]

When I asked God to make my black heart white as just a wee girl, my aim became to store my treasure in heaven and not in things on earth, which eternally will have no value.

The thought of storing your treasure comes from the Bible where Jesus told us to "store up for yourselves treasures in heaven"[6]. He linked this command to the desire of our hearts: "Where your treasure is, there your heart will be also[7]".

When we live sacrificially for Jesus' sake or serve Him by serving the body of Christ, the church, we store up treasure

[5] With permission from Mr Jim Crooks

[6] Matthew 6:20 NIV

[7] Matthew 6:21 NIV

in heaven. Even seemingly small acts of service do not go unnoticed by God. "If anyone gives even a cup of cold water to one of these little ones who is My disciple, truly I tell you, that person will certainly not lose their reward[8]".

There is a lovely hymn, the first time I heard it sung was at the Church of God in Kilsyth. At Christmas time they would put on musical concerts and it was one of the highlights of the year. In the choir my cousin Alex and his wife Helen, who you will read about later, would have sung this:

Cups of cold water, given in Jesus name,

Cups of cold water are never given in vain,

One day in heaven when we see the Lord,

Cups of cold water will bring their own reward.

I made it very clear to Ian that in my life God came first and if I had to make a choice between my business, my faith and how I practised it then the business would have to go, there was no contest. Ian, like so many people, worked hard and built up his business. He had built his own house, his only son had no interest in the business and his wealth for which he had worked so hard would have no impact on where he would spend eternity. What a waste. Can you just think for a moment, do a wee "stock take". Where are you in the "storing of your treasure"? Is it getting banked in heaven where it will have value for eternity or is it in an earthly bank or property, it has often been said "a shroud has no

---

[8] Matthew 10:42 NIV

pockets" another well-known saying is "the only two sure things in life are death and taxes[9]", two statements which are hard to disagree with.

Steep learning curve!

It was very hard to take over the business without Ian's guidance but others in the industry rallied and helped to support and encourage us. Clearly I could not do all the work myself and I employed people to help with collecting, grading and packing the eggs. Staff were also responsible for feeding and cleaning out the hens and we hired van drivers. The administration side was another aspect that had to be juggled, there were tele-sales asking for orders, planning delivery routes, purchasing supplies and counting up the cash float taken on the van run, as well as accounts and VAT forms. I hired a secretary to help in the office.

We expanded the delivery runs and at one point had three vans out delivering to as far as Aberdeen in the North, Dunbar in the South-East, Pitlochry, and Glasgow in the West. Not to mention various other places in between. Driving all over Scotland I soon became familiar with "short-cuts" and parts of towns I wouldn't otherwise have visited. Within the family it was often joked that Mum couldn't go anywhere in the car without having eggs for someone. One Christmas day we were invited to my brother and his wife's house. That Christmas morning the phone rang and it was a customer in Kirkcaldy. Well, we *were* passing, and they *were*

---

[9] Benjamin Franklin (1706-90), in a letter to Jean-Baptiste Leroy, 1789, which was re-printed in The Works of Benjamin Franklin, 1817

needing eggs! The eggs were packed amongst the Christmas presents and a slight detour was taken. Another time we were heading to Glasgow Airport for a flight to Italy to visit my sister and her husband. The suitcases were strategically packed so that the fifteen dozen eggs would remain intact en-route and be easily off-loaded to a small boy who was part of our "Eggs on Legs" team and whose mother worked in Renfrew, near the airport at Glasgow.

I should at this point explain that "Eggs on Legs" was part of our business. We encouraged older children and teenagers to earn their pocket money delivering our products around their local area. As well as the eggs, we sold bacon, cheese, yogurts, milkshakes, and bags of penny sweets. Some showed great entrepreneurial talent and became very organised expanding their customer base and showing great conscientiousness. In fact, I wrote job references for many of them and was delighted to do so. As it turned out my daughter later married one of our "Eggs on Legs" boys, who grew into a very responsible young man and has progressed well in his career path. Think that the credit for that should go to his parents and not the fact he was an "Eggs on Legs" lad!

"You don't have to be mad to work here, but it helps!"

Our staff bought a sign with this quote on it for our office. It was a tongue-in-cheek reference to the desk in my office. My filing system was once referred to as, "deep litter".

Deep litter is an animal housing system, based on the repeated spreading of straw or sawdust material in indoor booths. An initial layer of litter is spread for the animals to use for bedding material and to defecate in, and as the litter is soiled, new layers of litter are continuously added by the farmer. In this fashion, a deep litter bedding can build up to depths of 1-2 metres.[10]

It is true that my paperwork can be a mountain but I maintain that I know where everything is. Being too organised really wouldn't suit me. As such, staff coming to work with me had to be prepared to put up with my "madness"!

My Grandpa worked until he was seventy years old, then he retired. Family legend tells that after a few weeks at home with my Gran, who was fifteen years his junior, my Dad was brought in for a wee word, "George, can you get your father a job? He's driving me mad!" My Gran was longsuffering, but it seems a few weeks of "retirement" were enough! Dad sent one of his lorries to pick Grandpa up in the morning and he worked in the paving slab factory weighing in the delivery lorries to ensure Dad wasn't getting short changed in materials. He would make the men's tea in time for their break and generally kept the place tidy and swept up. Only when he physically was struggling to get into the lorry did he finally say to Dad, "I think I'd better call it a day Geordie". So when I was employing people there was no risk of ageism; I had been set a fine example in my Grandpa Machray.

---

[10] Groenestein & Van Faassen, 1996 - Volatilization of Ammonia, Nitrous Oxide and Nitric Oxide in Deep-litter Systems for Fattening Pigs. J. agric. Engng Res. vol. 65, pp269 – 274

At the end of the war my Uncle Stewart was in Berlin, as an army medic, he was sent to work in a hospital in Berlin alongside a Doctor who was doing ground breaking work with epilepsy. It would be years later when Uncle Stewart went to work at Quarrier's Homes[11] that he took the knowledge and inspiration gleaned from this forward thinking doctor and applied it to benefit his Scottish patients. God had prepared him for the job in Quarrier's long before Uncle Stewart knew he would be working there. It was generally known as the "Epileptic Colony" although it was originally named "The Colony of Mercy". It didn't open until after William Quarrier's death in 1903. In this day and age "Epileptic Colony" sounds awful, but the name is less important when you consider that in those days they were pioneering. At that time there were few drugs to control epilepsy, those in existence weren't as refined or as effective as today's medications. Those suffering from this awful illness would have seizures and all that could be done was to make them comfortable and safe until the seizure passed.

Lack of medical advancement in those days meant that there wasn't an understanding of the cause of the symptoms. This meant that it was assumed that sufferers of epilepsy couldn't work. Uncle Stewart went out to local industries and found real jobs that his patients could do. It had been unheard of to allow them to use machines and tools, but this innovative unit forged the way which helped to change attitudes. Sometimes the machines were brought to the workshop from the nearby car factories at Hillington. They could manufacture some of the smaller car

---

[11] http://www.workhouses.org.uk/Quarriers/

components. Many also made things such as trays, stools, baskets etc. I have vivid memories of going to the "workshop" and watching the workers take great pride in their craftsmanship. Some had been brain damaged after years and years of seizures. I remember they always welcomed me and were so happy to have visitors to admire their products. On reflection this was another linchpin in my inclusion background. This influence led me to be one of the first employers in the area to work with Fife Council as part of a new endeavour to employ those with additional needs.

During the egg years, we also had two children who daily came to the farm with their Mum and Gran. The ladies worked with us and along with our own Daniel we had a ready-made mini nursery, long before childcare provision was considered beneficial to businesses. I didn't see ourselves at the time as being at the forefront of these matters, it was just how we tried to accommodate people with varying needs. I couldn't have managed the business without their help.

Lecturer – for the blink of an eye

As I already stated, David worked at Elmwood College, which had a large agricultural department. By this time he was a team leader and responsible for organising the classes and curriculum. The college had a large "additional needs" department. At times it was challenging to provide appropriate placements for the students. I was enlisted as a temporary lecturer which involved me collecting the students from the college and bringing them to the farm.

I was responsible for two main groups. The first group could be described as having behavioural issues. It was my responsibility to instruct them on how to become good employees, and to encourage them with some of their core skills. They were involved in collecting the eggs and packing them. Unfortunately their enthusiasm was only for driving a tractor, which was not on the list of skills I was permitted to teach. This gave me the opportunity to highlight something which I have tried to impart to my own children. In every line of work there are things you like to do, and things you would prefer not to have to do. A good employee with a degree of maturity will complete all the required tasks. I mentioned to them that perhaps they were just not mature enough and was almost trampled by the rush of volunteers towards the least preferred jobs!

Two lads in particular were quite troublesome. I am five foot nothing and they were over six feet tall. Nevertheless over the weeks that we worked with them we seemed to "click". We practised core skills such as handling money and for their last session we held a Farmers' Market in the College reception area. They had a rota and these lads stayed on beyond their allotted time because they wanted to "help me out".

The other group were mostly young autistic adults. Some had no vocabulary at all. It was lambing time on the farm and we had "pet" lambs. They found packing the eggs more difficult so we would feed the pet lambs and then take a walk around the farm talking about things, escorted by our collie, Misty. Misty has always been a unique dog. She came to us as a pup. Those who train sheep dogs are very particular that you don't play with them because it can spoil them for their working life. But being in a home with four children it was inevitable that they would play with her, much to David's disgust. We need not have worried. Misty always had, and still has at the time of writing, the ability to switch from play-mode to working-mode in an instant. One of the youngsters picked up a large plastic lid and threw it like a Frisbee. Misty, happy to oblige, retrieved it and brought it back to the youngster. He threw it again and by this time the others in the group wanted to play the game. Some were shouting, "Misty, Misty!" and she would deliver the toy to them, they would take their turn. Then we realised that she also returned the toy to those who couldn't speak and shout her name, ensuring that everyone in the group had a fair turn. Initially I thought I had imagined it, then one of the support workers who came with the group said that she had realised this is what Misty had done. I had to agree with her. We later heard that one of the lads who had never spoken a word in his life went home to his mother and said the word, "dog".

Sepra

SEPRA stands for The Scottish Egg Producer Retailers' Association. It was formed in 1970 by a core group of producers who saw the benefit in working together to retail their eggs. As an egg producer it is impossible to have all the right sizes in the quantities which are required. Sometimes you have a surplus and sometimes a deficit. The British Egg Marketing Board had dealt with this but it was disbanded and so SEPRA was formed. By bringing Scottish egg producers together, it was possible to form an egg exchange within the association to enable a base price to be established. This proved to be most successful and continues today.

SEPRA also acts as a collective voice for the Scottish Egg industry and collaborates with the Scottish and UK governments independently through its membership of the British Egg Industry Council. The association produces weekly market reports complete with current egg pricing information for members and enjoys wide ranging expertise relating to the industry such as market trends, organic production, food, poultry welfare, hygiene and health, retail standards and supply chain management.

I was made aware of SEPRA and we became members. I attended the SEPRA meetings and I was then invited onto the Committee. I have often joked it was only because I attended all the meetings. I can't give you the timescales but it seemed only a short time passed and I was taken on as Vice Chairperson. I had no experience of being on a committee but I was passionate about hens and eggs and realised that it was better to be at the fore and have input. I couldn't sit back and allow things to happen especially if those "things" were potentially bad for the consumer, the hen or the producer.

BEIC meetings

SEPRA sent a representative to the British Egg Industry Council meetings held in London, there were about four per annum and The Chairperson or Secretary (Dennis Surgenor) would usually attend. It was decided that I should travel to

London with Peter Calder the then Chairperson. My flights were arranged, I was given the times of the flight from Edinburgh and the address of the hotel in London where the meeting would take place, there was no need for me to know how to get there as Peter Calder had been before and knew the route, he would accompany me.

I carefully chose what I would wear (first impressions and all that) and thought "how can a former nurse, wife, mother and egg farmer 'look the part' "? So I wore the smartest suit I had. I carried a brief case, which could have had a marmalade sandwich in for all anyone knew, if I'd had a trilby hat I may have been taken for Paddington Bear, all that was missing was a label saying, "please look after Moira"!

I wrapped up in a dressy trench coat, which had been bought for a "meet the industry" event at The Royal Highland Show. This event allowed us to network with representatives from the supermarkets. I was mingling with the many people and before I would speak to anyone I would examine their name badge to see which supermarket they were from. Imagine my surprise when I peered closely at the lapels of one suit unable to locate the name badge. I looked up into the face of none other than Prince Philip who was the main guest! Either the security man was sleeping or he deemed I posed no threat but I was definitely "up close" before I beat a hasty retreat as my colleague struggled to contain his hysteria.

Anyway, I digress again; my London trip was all planned but I was about to have one of the many "coincidences" I have had in my life, I believe they would be better described as "God-incidences".

I arrived for one of the early morning flights to London Heathrow leaving from Edinburgh that morning. I had not really had the chance to chat much to Peter Calder and was looking forward to the journey there and back and prayed that I might have the opportunity to tell him about my faith. When I got into the airport building there was no sign of Peter Calder. Edinburgh airport was much smaller back then, I think it was in the process of being extended as we were in a small check in area. The area was filled with people, most seemed to be in their own "wee world". I would later learn the "unwritten" rules that seem to be in the world of business travellers, these include the following: eye contact is seldom made, you chat to your colleagues but don't interact with other travellers. Suddenly a wave of insecurity swept over me and it would have been very easy just to turn around and slip away.

Then I spotted a "kent" (known) face. George Baird had been David's head of department at Elmwood College and was also a Christian. He spotted me too and came across to me, "What are you doing here, Moira?" I explained I was now vice-chair of SEPRA and I was on my first trip to the meeting in London. He was heading to Albania as part of a Church group to help there. We chatted and after a while he said, "Moira if you are getting this flight you'll need to check in". I tried to phone Peter but his phone was switched off, we had mobiles now, communication had advanced but it doesn't work unless they are switched *on*! I called his home and his wife assured me that he had left for the flight. I did worry if he'd had an accident en-route. I didn't know what to do, I didn't know where I would go when I got to Heathrow but decided there was no point in losing the ticket. I'd go to Heathrow and then decide what to do next when I got there. I went to the desk and they checked me in.

As I boarded the plane another wave of anxiety gripped me but I was quickly reassured when I saw George Baird sitting in the row in front of me. I settled down into my seat and got my seatbelt on, I listened attentively to the security instructions while most around continued reading and others were already grabbing a few extra forty winks. I did feel for the stewardess as she went through her well-practised routine and I tried to look as interested as I could to make up for the others around who were ignoring her directions. My thoughts turned to my destination and what I was going to do when I got to Heathrow. I also started to have a bit of a grump at God, after all I had great intentions of having a good conversation with Peter Calder, and how was I to do that if he wasn't even on the flight?

Some of the business travellers started to pull bits of paper out of folders and cases. My case had been securely stowed away in the overhead locker by a kindly businessman so was inaccessible. I made a short mental note to remember always to keep some documents handy to read en-route. I was sitting in the middle seat, on my right was a sleeping young man who looked as if he was travelling the world and smelt as if he hadn't had time for a shower since he left home six months before! On my left was a man in his mid-thirties who seemed very adept at balancing several documents, eating a snack and scribbling notes on the edges of the pages. Again my mind started to whirl. "Lord what will I do when I get off this plane? Help me to know what to do." I prayed, silently of course, I'm sure it would have caused a stir if I had prayed audibly!

My eyes were drawn to the papers being read by the man to my left, I couldn't believe it, the word "eggs" jumped out the page and hit me between the eyes! I looked straight forward, "get a grip, Moira! You're starting to see things, early morning starts obviously disagree with you!" I shut my eyes for a few minutes and then I thought, "look again and see what he is reading." Not only was the word "eggs" there but "hens" too. My heart started to race, you see the Egg Industry is relatively small and I didn't think there would be that many meetings being held in London involving eggs, certainly not on the same day. I took a deep breath, took the bull by the horns and turned to the man on my left saying, "Excuse me, I can't help noticing you are reading about eggs, I'm involved with the Scottish Egg Industry and I'm travelling to London to a meeting with the BEIC." "Really?" he replied looking quite startled "I'm Peter Logie, I represent the NFUS (National Farmers Union Scotland) and I'm going to that meeting too." I couldn't believe it, overwhelmed by relief, a fountain of explanations and requests came cascading out, "Oh, can you take me there?" and I began to explain how Peter Calder had missed the flight, and that this was not only my first visit to a BEIC meeting but also my first time travelling to London alone. I had the address of the hotel but no idea how to get there. Peter Logie said he would be delighted to take me but he was meeting another chap off the Aberdeen flight, would I mind waiting until we met up with Peter Chapman? I knew his brothers Robert and Derek, I bought hen and duck eggs from them. I told you it was a small industry! I certainly had no problem with waiting for the Aberdeen flight, after all I had no "plan B". Peter Logie then pulled out his diary and turning to the page which shows the underground routes he started to explain to me the route we would take. My mind wasn't taking any of it in.

I tried to look interested and pay attention but it was not a big diary and not that legible. I really couldn't see the small writing naming the stations and the coloured lines which merged and crossed like some kind of cross between Monopoly and Snakes and ladders. I thanked the Lord for looking after me and tried hard again to focus on what Peter Logie was saying.

I wondered at the odds of all the travellers on all the planes that left for London that morning from Edinburgh that I would be sitting in the seat next to the only other person traveling to London from Edinburgh to attend the same meeting as I was? Amazing! A "God-incidence". What would a statistician make of the odds of this coincidence? You couldn't make it up!

We met Peter Chapman off the Aberdeen plane and when he heard the story he said "That was a miracle." I beamed and said, "Yes but I have the God of Miracles looking after me and He knew I couldn't handle getting from Heathrow to the meeting without help." The two men then guided me up and down escalators, on and off busy trains and undergrounds, one in front to lead the way and the other behind to ensure I didn't get separated, instructing me on some more of these unwritten travellers' rules such as when travelling on the escalators you stand on the right to allow those who want to proceed more quickly to pass you on the left.

We arrived at the very grand hotel and, still sandwiched between my two chaperones, I almost followed Peter Logie into the "Gents"! A firm hand on my shoulder stopped me and a gentle Aberdeenshire lilt suggested I try the "Ladies".

We were all in fits laughing and were getting strange looks from the other guests in this five star London Hotel.

The meeting started, I felt decidedly nervous and like a fish out of water, however I remembered about my body language and hoped that by sitting forward on my seat and having an intense look on my face, whilst pausing to take notes I might at least "look" as if I knew what they were talking about! My teachers who had put on the productions at school would, I think, have been impressed.

About half way through Peter Calder arrived looking harassed and embarrassed; he mouthed a "sorry" across the table. He would later reveal that the flight schedule had been changed by fifteen minutes and he hadn't checked the ticket so he missed the plane but was able to get the next flight down. At the end of the meeting he came over full of apologies. Still flanked by my two guides who told him the whole story. Peter Calder said, "That was a miracle!" They both smiled and simultaneously replied, "Oh, don't worry about Moira, she has the God of Miracles looking after her!" I had planned to speak to Peter Calder, but God had a better and bigger plan. From what initially appeared to be a mess and a disaster, God brought a situation where everyone attending the BEIC meeting that morning heard what had happened and knew that I trusted in God. My colours were firmly "nailed to the mast" no going back now.

Chairperson – that's the gaffer, not the boy that hauds the chairs!

A couple of years later I was asked to become chairperson of SEPRA. There had been a steep learning curve not only with sheep but now hens and eggs. I really appreciated the value of eggs, nutritionally and for their convenience. They are a great source of inexpensive protein. They have been described as "Nature's convenience food" already packed in their own "container" and eggs have also been described as the perfect food as they are packed with protein, vitamins, minerals and "good" cholesterol. They have received a bad press on this last fact but recent research has now revealed there to be two types of cholesterol "good" and "bad". Eggs contain "good" cholesterol. I was passionate about animal welfare; about whether the hens were housed in cages, barn or free range, about telling the public about what a great industry we had in the UK and how well regulated we are. I knew getting the message out there was important.

I travelled more frequently to London. To start with I was accompanied by Dennis our secretary. Dennis "*was*" SEPRA. He worked tirelessly to ensure the weekly news sheet with prices went out as well as too many things to say here. Dennis was one of the founder members and his passion has not stopped even due to ill health.

I became quite adept at finding my way around London. SEPRA was self-funding and as I got more confident, I would to try to get the best prices for my flights, I also tried different routes. Then I discovered "Bargain Berths", on the overnight sleeper train, which were particularly good in the winter months. There is nothing glamorous in getting up at 4.30am to scrape the frost off the windscreen. In the low season, if you timed it well you could buy a sleeper berth on the Caledonian Sleeper service from Leuchars right into London for £20! For me this meant a short drive to the train station at Leuchars (free parking), hop on the train and into jammies- a wee cuppa, a read and gently be rocked into a, hopefully, deep sleep. It was quite comfortable if you let your body relax and let yourself go with the movement of the train, it reminded me of when I was a wee girl and I would fall asleep in the car, I was aware of the movement but totally trusted the driver to get me to my destination. Morning came with a gentle knock on the door and the attendant would hand in a breakfast bag with a cup of tea or coffee, really rather civilised! A quick tidy up at the little sink in the cabin and I stepped off the train much more refreshed than had I plumped for the 4.30am start and flight from Edinburgh Airport.

I remember one morning heading to the Airport going through my very well-rehearsed early morning routine. I would get up, put my heated rollers on to warm, go out and start the car, come back in to have some cereal and put my rollers in. I would keep them in until close to the airport when I would take them out with one hand whilst steering with the other. When I stopped a quick spray of hairspray and I was ready for business. It was never too much of a problem as very few other cars were on the road at that time of the morning and often it was dark so no one could see me driving with my curlers in, however one morning I was approaching Kirkcaldy when all the vehicles were being stopped by the police! I informed them I was heading to the airport for a flight to London and was allowed to carry on but not before the officer reminded me that it would be a good idea to take out my rollers! I have no doubt I would have been the cause of some jokes back at the station that day.

SEPRA promoted itself to those in the egg industry and also aimed to educate the public at The Royal Highland Show, an annual four day Agricultural show held near the airport at Edinburgh. The Show is well attended by those involved in agriculture and the wider public too. School children especially attend on the Thursday as schools find it a great destination for their annual school trip.

One year we had a competition for children who had to answer some questions such as "should you store an egg point down or point up?" the correct answer, by the way, is point down. Have you ever noticed a wee white stringy bit in your egg? This is the egg's "shock absorber". Didn't I say it was gobsmacking how they were produced? If the egg is stored point down then the shock absorber holds the yolk suspended in the middle of the white. This means that if bacteria gets through the shell then the yolk, where all the nutrients are, is surrounded by the white and the natural antibacterial properties have a chance to protect it. Don't ask me why they make fridges with storage for eggs where they have to lie on their sides, this is NOT how to store eggs.

While I'm on the subject, should eggs be kept in the fridge at all? We are the only European country to have the consumer advice "Keep refrigerated" on egg packaging. Everywhere else in Europe it is "keep cool". I think some wee translator got a bit over enthusiastic and before it was picked up it had been adopted into our legislation so we are stuck with it! If you keep them in the fridge, they can get moisture on the shell and then when taken into a warm kitchen you are providing ideal circumstances for bacteria to grow if not used immediately.

We also produced a comic for the show called "The Cackleberry News", cartoons were drawn by a friend who was a cartoonist. The idea was to get the message across about imports coming in from countries who didn't have the same standards as the UK as well as other welfare misconceptions. It was a bit of fun but hopefully got the message through.

Another year we had a cookery demonstration where Clarissa Dickson Wright (one of the Two Fat Ladies and sadly no longer with us) came and made omelettes. There were two stacks of eggs, one cage produced and the other Free Range. The concept was to find out which eggs produced the "best" omelettes. It truly was a "blind test" as I was the only one on the stand who knew which pile were from which system, and I wasn't telling until the end! Clarissa made an omelette from one side and the gathered audience tasted it, then she made an omelette from the other and they were asked to compare and say which they thought was from the Free Range. Even I was surprised and over eighty-five per cent of those gathered around chose the caged eggs as being better and thought they were from Free Range hens.

"Only The Shell Can Tell."

The EU brought in legislation that all eggs should be printed with the unique code of the egg producer and the system from which the egg came.

This was going to be yet another expense for producers to cover, we had already had heavy expense due to changes of legislation relating to the cage sizes. Please don't misunderstand me I have no problem if there is scientific proof to warrant changes but this seemed to be missing and there was no scientific basis for the change in cage sizes. Also the UK implements all changes in regulations from the EU, they "Gold Plate", which means going above and beyond what is required by law, and we have inspectors who police the regulations. There are other EU countries who blatantly ignore the regulations. This puts the UK at a marketing disadvantage.

It was suggested that we turn the printing of the eggs into a marketing advantage. We had for many years been trying to market Scottish eggs as a brand or at least to be able to state that they were produced in Scotland and this had been blocked. SEPRA asked the EU if we could use "SCO" to identify that the eggs had been produced in Scotland and they gave us permission to do so. Help was given by an experienced marketing company and the "Only The Shell Can Tell" slogan was born. In addition to the producer code and a number which identifies if the eggs were produced from: Free Range system (1), Barn (2) or cage (3) the customer can look for "SCO" as only the shell can tell if the egg has been produced in Scotland. We had a cartoon egg with a kilt called "McSepra". Watch out as McSepra may be making an appearance again soon.

Ross Finnie, the then Minister for Agriculture, launched the "Only The Shell Can Tell" campaign at the Royal Highland Show. The weather was poor and it had rained for days. This was a major problem as we only had an outdoor spot on a supplier's stall which had been kindly loaned to make the launch. My family were helping and we made our way in two cars with kilts and smart attire for the launch, one of our cars broke down on the way to the show ground so everything had to be transferred into the one car and we all squeezed in and put the pedal to the floor - we were running late! We parked and if you are reading this and have been to the show you will know there is usually quite a hike to get from the car park and into the show ground. We had the kilts and other bits and bobs and with umbrellas up battled towards the stand. Still unsure how we could make this launch with sheets of rain driving into the stand I was concerned that all the work and effort and money spent would be to no avail, however in a "you couldn't make it up" moment as Mr Ross Finnie stepped onto the stand the clouds parted. The sun shone for the time of speeches, the launch, and the photographers' session and as he stepped off the stand the clouds came over and hid the sun for the rest of the day, it was a definite answer to prayer.

Food Standards Agency

As I continued to attend the London BEIC (British Egg Industry Council) meetings it came to our attention that the Food Standards Agency wanted to carry out another survey on eggs for Salmonella. Hens were routinely being vaccinated against Salmonella and there hadn't been a review since the Edwina Currie debacle in 1988/1989.

For those of you who are too young to recall, there was a survey carried out. The finding was that one in every five hundred and sixty eggs was contaminated with salmonella.

This caused a food scare which resulted in producers having to dump eggs by the tonne. Many went out of business and some even committed suicide due to the pressures.

There was no issue within the industry over the new survey being done but when we were then told of the protocol: how they were going to carry out the survey and test the eggs, we did have grave concerns on several fronts. Food Standards have an "open and transparent" policy and on the whole this is admirable but within the egg industry we had members who had been targeted by Animal Rights Activists, some had even had their premises bombed. Many SEPRA members whom I represented lived on their farms, it had been made clear that there would be "naming and shaming" if eggs were found to have salmonella. We were very concerned that this would make some of our members and their families targets for some less rational individuals and there was a very real risk that someone could or would be injured. It is worth noting that during the first scare there were more farmers committed suicide than people died from Salmonella food poisoning.

The way the eggs were to be tested was also concerning. As I said, I came into the egg industry at the time of Mrs Currie's debacle and wasn't aware of the details of the previous testing. We were told that Food Standards Agency wanted to carry out the survey under the same conditions as fifteen years before to get a "like for like" comparison. That sounded sensible until I realised that to test the eggs they would smash the whole egg, shell and contents and test the mixture. I couldn't believe it. Firstly, no one deliberately eats egg shell and secondly knowing where an egg comes out from the hen the risk of salmonella contamination on the shell would have been considerably higher than the risk to the contents.

I repeatedly stated at meetings that these concerns needed addressed and the reply was always that Food Standards Agency would not discuss the matter. Then an invitation came from Food Standard Agency to a meeting of industry, the supermarkets and other interested parties. We were assured that there would be management present who would listen to our concerns and have the ability to make changes if required.

I planned my journey carefully as this meeting would be held at the Food Standard Agency building in London. Now, I was by this time quite comfortable traveling to the BEIC offices, but this was a new destination so I was a bit anxious. During this time I was also running around the countryside as both my Dad and David's Mum were unwell. My Dad was two hours away on the West coast of Scotland and David's Mum was two hours away South of us. I was juggling running the business and family life too. The meeting was to be held on my birthday in January but thankfully it was late morning so there was no need for a 4.30am start.

I arrived at Edinburgh airport relatively relaxed as I had researched the route and knew where I was going. I was quite a different Moira from the one who had arrived at the same airport several years before as Vice-Chair. I was more confident and no longer relied on "looking" the part as I felt I could do the part. Often in these business meetings there seemed to be a lack of common sense and although I didn't have a degree in poultry husbandry, (or in anything for that matter!) I did have common sense and also a focus on solving problems. The latter possibly related to my dyslexia as to overcome the disability, strategies are developed whether purposefully or unintentionally.

I had been reading in the book of Proverbs, a book in the Bible written by Solomon a very wise King. Many of these proverbs were running round my head as I went through the now familiar routine of checking in for my flight. These were the days before "on-line" check in facilities. As I waited in the queue I became aware of those before me turning with frustrated looks on their faces but I couldn't hear what had been said by the Airline passenger service assistant to cause their frustration. Then it was my turn. The neatly turned out lady with immaculate makeup and hair gently swept back into a French Roll smiled wryly as I presented her with my passport for Identification and my printed ticket, "Ah, yes, you are traveling to Gatwick? Well I'm sorry to tell you that the plane has had a mechanical breakdown and it is stranded in London, we are getting a replacement but there will be a three hour delay." My heart sank, if I waited for the replacement flight I would miss the meeting. There were other flights available to other airports but not with the same airline. I would have to purchase another ticket and buying them on the spot always made them more expensive. I was frustrated, I couldn't make this decision myself, it was SEPRA money and not for me to spend without discussion. I quickly phoned Dennis, his wife Muriel answered the phone. Dennis wasn't available to come to the phone, there was no time to wait. A decision had to be made. Now Muriel wasn't on the committee but she was as much involved as anyone on the committee and supported Dennis fully in his involvement in the egg industry. That said, Muriel and I took an "executive decision" and I rushed back to the appropriate desk and purchased another ticket.

However, now I was going to Heathrow and I had no route planned to get to my destination. I had to run to get to the gate and board as the flight was departing soon. Now we had mobile phones but they were not "smart" phones so I couldn't refer to "google maps" to help me find my way.

As I sat on the plane, I was thinking about the Proverbs that I had been reading, some related to good advice and the timing of it, timing was very tight especially as I wasn't sure how long it would take from Heathrow to the FSA offices. I had been praying that God would help me get to this meeting if that was what He wanted me to do, and that He would guide me as to what to say to break down this seemingly immoveable barrier there was between the FSA and the industry.

When I got off the plane I ran as quickly as I could with my "I mean business" suit and high heels. It was a Jaeger suit which I would not normally have been able to afford. I had purchased it in a sale when invited to attend a meeting in Brussels as Scottish representative for the European equivalent of the National Farmers Union. That was another "I can't believe I'm doing this" moment. It was a fine, light grey, wool suit which had a silver thread through it, the skirt was straight and short but not in an immodest way and the jacket was collarless, with concealed buttons and was beautifully cut so I felt ready to take on the "big boys". I added colour and warmth by throwing on one of my Bolivian Alpaca wraps, they were light weight and toastie warm. They could be a blanket or a pillow if rolled up so very flexible. I headed for the Express train which would take me into the centre of London.

As I sat on the train I decided that if I saw a taxi sign first, I would take a taxi but if I saw the underground sign first then I would take the underground although I would have to ask someone what station and "line" of the underground I needed to take, remember I was travelling with no plan. It made me thankful that in a broader sense I was travelling on the journey of life with a plan. The Bible says:

> *"For I know the plans I have for you," says the*
> *LORD. "They are plans for good and not for*
> *disaster, to give you a future and a hope."*
> *Jeremiah 29:11*

From the day I first began a relationship with God and He forgave my sins, I knew I was travelling on a path bound for heaven. That security and the knowledge that He is with me through all the twists and turns is a wonderful place to be. Do you have a plan for eternity?

I asked the Lord to guide me and help me, I got off the train and started to run again, time was of the essence and I had a sense of urgency whilst trying to maintain my business like appearance. Ahead I saw the sign: "TAXI". "Okay Lord, it'll be a taxi then!" I thought. Thankfully there was not much of a queue and within a few minutes of jumping off the train I jumped into the back of a taxi cab, gave the "cabbie" the address and sank into the soft leather seats of a Black London Taxi slowly starting to get my breath back.

The Cab driver with a thick "cockney" accent half turned his head and to make conversation asked if I was down to the City for business or pleasure. If I had been switched on I might have been offended that my carefully chosen attire didn't give him the clue that I was there on business, thankfully that point flew over my head. I explained to him that it was business. Now I had, at every opportunity, asked "the public" what part of the egg was tested for salmonella when it was the Mrs Currie scare, my chauffeur was not to escape my questioning. He laughed and with a few expletives said that it was probably the whole egg. Now this was not the standard answer, most would reply that they would test the part of the egg that we eat and would be surprised when I would inform them that it was the whole egg.

In between our conversation I was aware that the traffic was moving very slowly and started to have doubts if I had made the right decision about taking the taxi. I told him of my "mission" my concern that if the protocol wasn't changed then we would have another food scare and it would be the most vulnerable in our society that would suffer. I tested him out with some of my proverbs that were running round in my head. "Proverbs, that's a book in the Bible that has lots of good advice," he mused. It is well known that London cabbies are clever cookies and my driver was no exception. "You go to your meeting and set them straight, you can do it -you have confidence." My answer to him was that my confidence came from God and that He would help me. My driver announced that we had arrived and that the building I was looking for was just over the road. He had pulled up just outside an underground station but had I travelled by underground I would not have had the encouragement from my new found "friend".

I had to keep my wits about me as I dodged the traffic to get across the busy road. The Food Standards Agency is an independent department of the government which is responsible for food safety and hygiene across the UK. They work with businesses to help them produce safe food, and with local authorities to enforce food safety regulations. Their building in the UK capital had an impressive traditional curved stone frontage almost like an ancient monument but when you entered through the doors you were in what was a very impressive modern atrium. I was asked to take a seat and was kept waiting for about five minutes, this was more than a tad frustrating given the efforts I had taken to get to the meeting as quickly as possible, at this point I was about twenty minutes late. Finally a tall young man approached and asked me to follow him and he would take me to the meeting room. As I entered the lift I tried to gather my thoughts as to how I would be received and how I should "behave".

I slipped quietly into the room where the tables were set in an almost oval shape but with the straight "top table" spoiling the smooth line of the shape. I took the nearest available space and sat down, well not quite as I caught my shoe on the leg of the chair and half fell into the seat. I don't think too many noticed as the atmosphere was so tense you could have cut it with a knife. I looked across to see some of my colleagues from BEIC, their faces were tense and one chap's veins were pulsating on the side of his temples, I remember thinking, "Please don't have a heart attack. I don't want to have to resuscitate you in front of everyone!" Others, whom I didn't recognise and presume were representing the supermarkets, were equally tense. It didn't take long for me to realise that this meeting wasn't going well.

Waiting for an appropriate interlude I put my hand up to indicate to the Chairperson that I would like to speak. The Chairperson indicated that I could join the debate. Introducing myself first, I then apologised for my late arrival, briefly explaining the mechanical fault on the plane. I then continued to say that as I had been selected to be Chairperson for SEPRA I was acutely aware that I needed wisdom for the task. "You will all have heard of the wisdom of Solomon? Well Solomon wrote one of the books in the Bible called Proverbs. I have been reading them recently and Proverbs chapter twenty-five verse eleven tells us: 'Timely advice is as lovely as golden apples in a silver basket'. I hope that the advice I bring to this meeting today will be timely and fruitful and that we will have a good outcome for the consumers of the UK and for the producers who seek to feed the people." I'm not sure if they were shocked at the Bible being quoted but there was an easing of the tension. Further debate took place and the man sitting on my right, whom I later discovered was a statistician with FSA, tapped me on the arm and whispered "chuck another proverb at them!" I was taken aback and then suddenly the Chair brought the meeting to a close as she did so I said, "There is another proverb that says: 'A poor person's farm may produce much food, but injustice sweeps it all away'[12]. If this survey continues with the protocol unchanged then we will have another food scare and it will be the most vulnerable in our society who depend on the inexpensive source of protein in eggs who will suffer most. Farmers and their families will be put at risk too." I was glad that I was sitting down as my legs were like jelly and my knees positively knocking. The man to my right introduced himself and said, "Good on you!" Someone else stood behind me and whispered in my ear, "That is the first business meeting I have ever been in where the Bible was quoted, can I say

---

[12] Proverbs 13: 23 NIV

how refreshing it was." He had slipped away before I turned to see who had said it.

When I felt my legs had recovered sufficiently to allow me to stand and not repeat my entrance and flop back down, I stood up. There were little groups of people chatting and I headed to the person who had chaired the meeting. I complained to her that we had been assured that there would be people with the seniority to make changes and she had stated that this was not the case, we had been misled. She retorted by saying "Write to Sir John Krebs and stick your proverbs in it." Well I did write to Sir John who was the Chair of FSA at that time and I did put in some more proverbs. I didn't receive a reply immediately and then I received an invitation to attend the FSA on the 28th of February 2003 in the afternoon, 1.30pm, if my memory serves me right. Now what was particularly poignant about the timing of the meeting was that the survey was due to start the next day on the 1st of March. I had alerted the BEIC that we were being given a further opportunity to discuss matters further but they declined to be involved. Dennis then spoke with a representative, David Spackman, of UKEPRA. UKEPRA is a sister organisation to SEPRA but for the UK, they covered the rest of the UK and we had a good working relationship. David is a specialist poultry veterinarian and had the technical expertise that I didn't. As I said earlier I was dashing about the country seeing to ill parents. I also had a BEIC meeting on Wednesday the 26th, they were not happy about David Spackman and me meeting with FSA and felt we would make the matter worse, I couldn't see how it could be worse.

I flew back up to Edinburgh and was driving down to my parents in Gourock, Dad had just been discharged from hospital. He had been very ill and the family were taking turns to stay overnight with Mum and Dad. I received a phone call from my daughter to say one of my sons had been taken into hospital. He had been attacked at school a few days earlier and he had deteriorated leading to his admission. They assured me everything was under control and that I should continue to care for Mum and Dad. The next morning I headed for the hospital in Dundee, there was a possibility that surgery might be required. We waited the whole day then thankfully after a scan it was decided that the operation would be postponed and he would be treated conservatively. I said I would cancel the meeting with FSA in London the next day and was told by my son, in no uncertain terms, to get to London and "sort them out!"

I wearily drove back to Gourock, my flight was booked from Glasgow so it made sense to keep to the original plan. I remember very clearly sitting in the bedroom at Mum and Dad's flat, it was about midnight and I was physically and mentally exhausted. I cried out to God as I felt overwhelmed by the events past and the meeting to come. I lifted my Bible and silently said, "Lord, I need a verse." My Bible fell open and my eyes fell on these words, *"I am the LORD and I do not change."*[13] Suddenly my heart was lifted as I thought about difficult, yes, even impossible situations that God's servants had found themselves in the past and how God had strengthened them and many miracles occurred. I thought of David going to fight Goliath and felt my situation was like David (me) going to face Goliath (FSA). I drifted into a peaceful sleep and in the morning felt refreshed, it wasn't

---

[13] Malachi 3:6 NLT

an early flight. This time the flight was on time and my journey uneventful.

I met David Spackman and we went in together. As we sat in the modern atrium waiting to be taken up to the meeting, we exchanged thoughts about the meeting, were we wasting our time, would we make things worse? I shared what had happened the day before and the verse God had given me for reassurance. As we went up in the lift my knees started to feel decidedly wobbly as a wave of anxiety washed over me. However, there was no time to let it take hold as we were taken into a smaller room this time and we were welcomed by Dr Andrew Wadge, who was the acting Director of the Food Safety Policy Group.

As I had requested the meeting, Dr Wadge invited me to commence proceedings and present my concerns. I briefly explained my nursing background and how I had come into the industry and repeated the concerns I had raised at the January meeting. Dr Wadge stated that as the main focus of FSA was consumer welfare and food safety he would agree to discuss the protocol and see where we could make improvements. I couldn't believe what I was hearing, my heart leapt in my chest but quickly I had to gather myself and "do the business."

We came out of the meeting and I couldn't believe what had just happened. They agreed to test the egg shell and contents and report the results clearly so the consumer would know how many eggs had shell contamination and how many internal contamination. The samples would be taken from the retail sector (shops, supermarkets etc.) If there was contamination on the shell alone then it would be unfortunate that the farmer would be held solely responsible as the contamination might *not* have taken place on the farm. It was agreed that if contamination was found there would be the possibility of further testing of eggs from that farm to identify if there was a problem on that unit. It was agreed that only if there was evidence of a problem on a unit would they be "named and shamed". It was also important to identify that the eggs had been produced in this country and were not ungraded imports as we knew that the continent had a much bigger problem with salmonella than we did.

There were a few more factors discussed and agreed and we couldn't have had a more successful outcome. The survey started the next day with the changed protocol. God had used a former nurse, housewife and Mum to have an impact on what was an independent organisation similar in size and with as much power as the government. I am thankful to David for coming with me; we were a good team. As I walked out onto that busy London street and David and I parted. I stopped for a moment just to savour what had happened. I thanked God for this amazing miracle and I looked at the crowds rushing by and thought, "You have no idea what has just happened and the impact it may have on you in a few months' time." The next few months went by and I continued to rush about the country. The FSA survey went on but there was no news, we had done all we could, all that remained was to be patient and wait for the result.

Howie-Surgenor – October 2003

October came around very quickly and it was time for the Annual Poultry Club dinner, held at The Dunblane Hydro. This was a highlight for those involved both in the poultry laying and poultry meat industries. These two faces of the poultry industries came together, and we caught up with old friends, had a lovely meal and enjoyed an after dinner speaker. One of the main highlights of the evening was the presentation of the Howie-Surgenor Cup. This was an award set up by Poultry producer and former Chairperson of SERPA, Tom Howie and the then current secretary Dennis Surgenor. The award was presented annually to someone who had made a major contribution to the poultry industry. The introduction of the award mimicked the introduction of "This is your life" a TV programme from the sixties and seventies, shrouded in secrecy before the evening there were only a very few who knew who the recipient of the award would be.

Prior to the event I had been tasked to get a gift to present to one of our former committee members, June, who was also my "feed rep" and friend, she was moving on to pastures new. June had received her presentation gift and returned to the table, the applauding had settled and the chair was moving on to the Howie-Surgenor cup presentation. I was trying to say to June that if she didn't like the jewellery then it could easily be changed and she could make the choice herself. She was trying to "shhhh" me and draw my attention to the next matter, the award. Suddenly, I heard the description of the recipient and realised I was the one being described. I had no idea it was to be me, June did though! I was then named and the reason given for being chosen for the award was the major contribution that I had made that year in particular with the FSA. David, my husband, had been in the loop and numerous surreptitious phone calls had been taking place to glean the background information, usually when I was visiting the Mums and Dads at either end of the country. In hindsight I should have twigged something was going on, after all David had gone and got a haircut for the event!

I was invited to the platform and presented with the cup, it was a very emotional moment. Those who know me well know that I hate surprises but I was whipped up like the big wave that the surfers enjoy and took to the crest of the wave with great delight, mingled with a little embarrassment. I knew of others who also gave a great deal to the industry and were more worthy of the accolade than I, around three hundred and fifty attendees were now settling in expectation and a hush fell over the room, they were waiting for an impromptu speech. What would I say, what could I say? Mrs Shaw, my old English teacher's words rang in my head, "always speak about what you know about". She had taught us in a very innovative way for her time and generation considering she was no "spring chicken". We would participate in "Just a minute" like the radio programme, where you have to speak on a given subject for one minute without repetition, hesitation or deviation. She would challenge us with topics known and less known and some positively obscure. We had class debates where we had to take both sides, encouraging us to think from the opposite side of the coin, a tact I used frequently in the "egg days" in particular. She encouraged us to be part of The Speech Society and I came second in the

Rotary Club annual competition when in second year at school.

In a matter of seconds I had to gather myself, reign in the emotions and present a speech. "Deep breath, drop your shoulders, make eye contact, smile and... start." Oh Mrs Shaw, I now appreciate what a good teacher you were! I thanked the audience and those who had chosen me for such a prestigious award. I can't remember too much of what I said, I do remember telling them that many Christians had prayed for our industry and the individual families who would be affected by the testing. I explained how God had guided me and intervened with the FSA. I told them the story that I have just told you and I remember adding, "Wouldn't it be wonderful if no salmonella was found either in or on any Scottish eggs, perhaps that is a miracle too much to ask for." I was the first and, up until 2014, the only woman recipient of the award. This record was to be broken in 2014 when joint recipients, Professors Sally Solomon, whom I spoke of earlier in this story, and Maureen Bain, both of Glasgow University, received the Howie-Surgenor Cup. They were far more worthy recipients than I. Sadly Sally passed away in February 2015.

It would be the following January 2004 before the results of the survey were revealed and they were amazing. Out of twenty-eight thousand five hundred eggs tested across the UK there were **none** found to have salmonella contamination in them and only nine eggs had salmonella on the shell. But wait for it... No *Scottish* eggs had salmonella either in or on them! Clearly it was not a miracle too much to ask for. You couldn't make it up! Did this wonderful news hit the headlines? Sadly it did not. There was always something more "news worthy" and despite the

FSA holding the story to try and get a suitable slot for a "good news" story, the public never got to hear the results of the survey.

"For everything there is a season, a time for every activity under heaven."[14]

Europe decided that the conventional cages would be banned in 2012 and there was a great push for Free Range units. There simply would not be sufficient suitable ground for all the free range birds required to produce eggs to feed the country and no safeguards to cage produced eggs still coming from other countries. I had been unwell with a Post Viral illness and various other circumstances were making me seriously consider my situation within the industry. I wasn't happy about changing to Free Range as our farm wasn't particularly suited to it and at that point there was very little talk of accepting the enriched cage system, that would also have involved a major investment and one I felt was a gamble. There would be no protection of our market and even in the EU from country to country legislation is adopted differently and many countries don't ensure that the legislation is being complied with. Also there were to be derogations (delays) for new member states so they could still produce under the current systems and market their eggs to us without the increased costs. Just at that time we received a letter from another egg producer offering to buy

---

[14] Ecclesiastes 3:1 NLT

the business. The timing was right and we accepted his offer.

Chapter 4: When the phone rings!

Not quite by Royal Appointment

It was about lunchtime on a Saturday when the phone rang. I had just come in from the egg packing shed, we collected the eggs everyday but only graded them Monday to Saturday so when the grading of eggs finished on the Saturday you had a feeling of taking a wee breath as another business week had passed.

The voice on the other end of the phone line had a hint of panic, albeit controlled, the Lady (yes it is correct with a capital "L") explained that she had been at the delicatessen in St Andrews and they didn't have any quails' eggs. Quail are very small birds and lay very small eggs, which are deemed to be a delicacy. The dilemma this Lady found herself in was that she was expecting Princess Margaret to stay for a few days and the Princess had particularly requested quails' eggs and there was none to be purchased.

Now, I must admit to start with I thought one of my staff was "winding me up", thankfully I had decided to "play along". I realised fairly quickly that this was a genuine call before I embarrassed both myself and this dear Lady. I explained that it was one of our staff who kept the quail and I would have to check with him if he had any available. A quick phone call established that there were one and a half dozen available and it was with great relief that the Lady said she would take them all if that was possible. I was instructed where to deliver them and informed that the back door would be open, money would be left on the kitchen table and I was to leave the eggs with a receipt on the table. There was a sigh of relief and an exchange of further pleasantries and I assured her that all would be well. Given the fact that I had to drive to pick up the eggs, then deliver them further along the beautiful East Neuk coast, time was short so I jumped in the Land Rover, still in my working clothes and headed off.

All went well, the eggs were collected and the instructions were followed. I found the house, a large mansion hidden behind a thick blanket of trees which opened into a large cleared area of beautifully kept gardens. Concealed in the beautiful Fife countryside this mansion house was perfectly located. The back door was indeed open and the money on the kitchen table, just as described. I placed the eggs and receipt on the table and took the money, making my way back to the Land-Rover. I placed the key in the ignition and as I turned the key lifted my eyes to see that the way was clear for a quick getaway. As I started the car to my horror a fleet of large black limousines appeared out of the trees and swept along the long curving drive towards me. At that point my concern was that my Land-Rover was not what you would describe as particularly clean, well, it *is* a work horse. I was to become more alarmed when the second car stopped just in front of my car, blocking off my escape route. The window was wound down and an arm appeared signalling me to approach the car. My appearance was not appropriate for such an encounter but there was absolutely nothing I could do. As I got closer the Lady who had called me was leaning over the driver to shake my hand and thank me profusely for coming to her rescue on a Saturday afternoon. I was conscious of two others in the back seat and as I glanced over the driver's seat saw that one of the occupants was none other than Princess Margaret herself.

Now my upbringing had in no way prepared me for such an encounter, as I was trying to exchange pleasantries with the front seat passenger I was processing the situation and trying to conclude what the appropriate etiquette should be. I had a vague recollection of hearing that you don't speak with Royalty until they speak to you, where I heard that was neither of any consequence nor importance in that brief moment of time. What was said was a blur, all I can remember is giving a "dip" as a half curtsy and a half squint smile and nod of the head by way of acknowledgement. I didn't want to be rude and ignore the Royal recipient of the very important quails' eggs. My attempts at royal protocol, I felt, failed miserably as my half smile was returned by what could only be described as a "Paddington Bear hard stare" and if you don't know what that means I suggest you need to read the stories about Paddington Bear as you have really missed out. Perhaps the occupants of the rear seat were in need of a cuppa after a long journey, I know I certainly was, after that very traumatic encounter. It was a relief when the few moments of time, which felt like an hour, were over and my customer allowed me to escape back to my dirty "Landy", hide my embarrassment and head for home with another "you couldn't make it up" story tucked under my belt.

Have you got a turkey?

Christmas always seems to come around very quickly and if you are a working Mum I'm sure you will agree with me that they seem to come all the more quickly. The chat over the egg grading machine and over coffee breaks was increasingly about what Christmas preparations had been done and what items were still on the "to do" list. In my case most were still on the "to do list"! The staff kept asking me, "have you got your turkey yet?" I would flip the question away with a, "*No,* but it's on the list". As always the list, somehow was done by Christmas Eve and the Turkey safe in the fridge. I was bustling about trying to complete the "cleaning" to do list, even though it was 9.30pm on Christmas Eve, when I was interrupted by the phone. This time it was a lady who was frantic and speaking so quickly I was having difficulty in following her, "have you got a turkey?" Ahh, I thought, this is one of the staff winding me up! "Yes," I replied, "I *have* a turkey." The relief in her voice was palpable over the phone, "can I come and pick it up?" she replied. "Sorry? It is *my* turkey I have!" I blurted out as the penny dropped that this was a genuine call. The woman burst into tears, it transpired she had bought a frozen turkey and had started to defrost it when the most pungent of smells started to permeate through her newly cleaned house. It was putrid and most definitely not fit for human consumption. My heart went out to her as I tried to think of anyone who might have a "spare" turkey. I explained that we were an egg production farm, quite different from turkey rearing and that most independent turkey rearers had closed due to the pressures from the supermarkets and now only reared to order. I did phone one that I knew of but they couldn't help. As we tucked into our turkey that Christmas, it stuck in my throat a bit as I thought of the family without. For several years after, I not only bought my turkey but always bought a second, just in case I ever got another phone call from a woman in distress on Christmas Eve.

As I'm remembering more phone calls I have taken over the years one of the most "you couldn't make it up" was one received from Norway. The deep soothing tone of what I imagined to be a very handsome man (simply from his voice!) asked the question, "Are you the Moira Henderson I met on the slopes of the Cairngorms in the 1950s?" For a moment I wished I had been, but I enlightened him that I had not even been a twinkle in my Dad's eyes in the 1950s. This Norwegian gentleman was searching for, what he had now discovered in his sixties, was the love of his life! He had been a ski instructor and had met and fallen in love with Moira Henderson. However, he wanted to see the world and left her behind to pursue what was to be a very adventurous and dangerous existence involving many countries of the world and numerous occupations, including mining for gold and being a mercenary soldier. He had taken the decision to phone every Moira Henderson in the UK phone book in a bid to trace her. These were the days before the World Wide Web and having so many helps to trace those with whom we have lost touch.

He was able to tell me she had been a school teacher and came from a particular area in the Scottish Highlands and her father was/had been a farmer. I thought perhaps we could place an advert in "The Scottish Farmer" in the hope someone would respond. Conscious that this lady's feelings toward this man who had dumped her for adventure might not be particularly welcoming, I took his phone number and said I would do what I could. He faxed me various newspaper clippings highlighting his adventures and an accident which cost him his arm and almost his life. Later that morning I was on the phone to egg producers who coincidentally were in the same area as the missing lady had come from. I was buying their surplus eggs from them as they were of very good quality. As I mused about the phone call I had received earlier the lady said, "I'll phone the local radio station and perhaps they will announce it on the radio." Less than two hours later my friend was back on the phone and "Moira" had been traced. Later in the day I received another phone call, this time from "Moira" and I explained how I had become involved. She told me that he had been her first love and how she was broken hearted when he left, it had taken many years to get over her broken heart but she had moved on and was now very happily married. She took the contact information he had given me and said she would speak to him or write.

I phoned "A" and he was blown over with the news that she had been traced and so quickly, he had been trying for over a year. He described me as an "Angel" and I laughed and said that my husband wouldn't agree with that, but added that I was a Christian and the Bible described me as "a saint." He said it was strange that I should mention that as he had been reading his Mother's old Bible, but as it was in "old" Norwegian he was having difficulty in understanding it. I said we had friends who were Christians in Norway and I would arrange for him to be given a more modern translation of the Bible.

It would be a few weeks later when the Norwegian man phoned again, Moira had been in touch, wounds had been opened and hopefully cleaned out with the view to healing and he appreciated that she had moved on and that he had been foolish to let her slip through his fingers. He had received the Bible and assured me that he was enjoying reading it. I never heard from him again although, I did "google" his name, years later and it came up with a newspaper story of an elderly man fighting for better financial support from the government and the image looked very like an older version of the man in the newspaper clippings sent to me from "A".

Chapter 5: Family – the ties that bind.

I was part of a fairly large family with lots of aunts, uncles and cousins. One Sunday night after visiting Gran and Grandpa Machray, there was another lady visiting and Dad gave her a lift home. She thanked "Uncle George" for the lift. I got a shock, she was my cousin and I didn't know her! She was the daughter of my Dad's oldest sister and was married with her own family. I was the "baby" of my Mum's family the Millers and the second youngest on the Machray side, so in all fairness some of my older cousins were married and having their own children before I even came along.

Both my grandmothers were very caring individuals, I often wonder, is there a gene for care and compassion or is this something that is learned? My Gran Miller was widowed at the age of fifty-two and was left to bring up her family of five sons and two daughters. Jack was the eldest, then Bert, Jimmy, Nora, Stewart, Ernie and my Mum, Margaret. Gran was known in the town for her wisdom and care. It is said that if someone had a difficulty in their locality they would send for Auntie Nelly, "she will know what to do". Nelly was the family's pet name for Eleanor as was "Nora". It has become a family name now, with each generation naming an Eleanor. First there's my sister and then our daughter is Ruth Eleanor and our eldest granddaughter is Beth Eleanor. As I write this book, Uncle Stewart, who I mentioned earlier, is the only surviving Miller of that generation. He is now ninety-nine years old and still has a smile which lights up the room. He had such an interesting life and many "you couldn't make up moments" too. He was a stretcher bearer in the Second World War and was mentioned twice in dispatches for rescuing people under fire. The Miller children were all active Christians and were such tremendous role models. I never met my Grampa Miller but he was a Godly man and I know they both prayed earnestly for their children and grandchildren. God has answered their prayers, all their children were committed Christians and an example to their own families.

Strangely I had two Aunt Marys on the Machray side of the family. As a child I thought my Gran must have liked the name "Mary" so much that she called two of her daughters by the same name! I have to laugh at how, as a child, I tried to make sense of this rather strange situation. I would then discover, when I was able to understand more, that my Gran and Grandpa had taken in a lodger, a young man with a new-born baby whose wife had tragically died in childbirth. My Gran brought up Mary Cameron as her own, she was one of the family, and to this day her children are our cousins and we keep in touch. When someone trusts in the Lord the Bible describes us as being adopted into the family of God. The example my Gran and Grandpa showed was that just as being adopted into the family of God, there is no difference in treatment, in belonging, each is equal in all matters.

Most of us did all get together at Christmas and New Year, at least the aunts and uncles and girlfriends and boyfriends of cousins, most of whom would later join our family. I loved these occasions, usually organised and hosted by my Mum and Dad, as our house was big enough for all to gather together. These were the days before freezers and I can remember the walk in pantry (a cool room or cupboard) would be groaning with lots of goodies. Crates of tangerines and grapes would be joined by apples often wrapped in tissue paper, bought at the fruit market in Glasgow to ensure freshness. The fridge too would have every *square inch* used, yes we used imperial measures in those days. There were large bowls of fruit salad and trifles with cream to drizzle over the top. Ice cream involved a special trip to the local Italian ice cream shop which had to be done just before we started our meal. Otherwise, it would have melted by the time we got to the third or fourth course, depending on what menu Mum had settled on. Massive pots of soup would be bubbling away on the Esse cooker that I spoke of earlier and my sister would stand for hours peeling and chopping the vegetables for soup and the veggies to go with the main course which would have to be the traditional turkey with all the trimmings.

My responsibility was setting the table, now there could be around twenty to twenty-five guests all sat down around a long table, which under the brilliant white starched linen table covers, was made up of several tables sitting end to end. Hand embroidered smaller table covers would be set strategically at an angle to help disguise the "joins" of the tables. As I had to use several sets, I took great care to ensure that the pattern on the forks matched that on the knives and spoons. I loved making the napkins into strange shapes a bit like origami. When we went out for a meal to a hotel, and that was not such a common occasion as it is now, I would ask the waiters to show me new ways of folding the white starched linen napkins. A consultation with Mum was required to determine which set of china would be used. She had several sets of china, certain sets would be used for one family and others for the other. I think there may have been a diplomacy issue as some had been given as gifts and so it was very important to show that they were being used as a sign of appreciation. Plates of butter would be strategically placed to ensure no one had to stretch too far to reach them. The same was the case for the salt and pepper sets, again which had to match, do you think I have a wee bit of Obsessive Compulsive Disorder? Bowls of beetroot and chutneys, usually homemade gave lovely colour and of course the Christmas Crackers with their hidden surprises added the, oh so important, festive splash.

Other family occasions such as weddings were great days of celebration and reinforced the importance of family to us all. One year, my sister was bridesmaid five times and at that time the traditional gift from the bridesmaid was the "Wedding china" usually a half tea set (six of everything) but Mum always made sure that a full set was given, this meant enough for twelve guests. Knowing the joy of a large family; Mum liked to encourage the next generation to entertain and give hospitality.

Many families in the fifties and sixties experienced the pain of separation when families emigrated, and our Miller family was no exception. So when that part of the family returned for holidays from their new home land, Australia, this was indeed a very good reason for celebration and of course a party. Aunt Nora would organise the games at the Miller parties, there were always balloons and bubbles involved and it is amazing how many games can be played with balloons. Uncle Ernie was the joker of the family and would have us in pain having laughed so much at his antics. Uncle Jimmy would join him and they would sing "silly duets" with

Uncle Ernie on the piano it would start off sounding quite serious and then dissolve gradually off tune but in a deliberate way. It almost sounded "right" but not quite right, Les Dawson must have followed their lead! I seem to remember "A wee cock Sparra"[15] being one of their repertoire.

A wee cock sparra sat on a tree,

Chirpin awa as blithe as could be.

Alang came a boy wi'a bow and an arra

And he said: 'I'll get ye, ye wee cock sparra.'

The boy wi' the arra let fly at the sparra,

And he hit a man that was hurlin' a barra.

The man wi' the barra cam owre wi' the arra,

And said: 'Ye take me for a wee cock sparra?'

The man hit the boy, tho he wasne his farra,

And the boy stood and glowered; he was hurt
tae the marra.

And a' this time the wee cock sparra,

Was chirpin awa on the shank o' the barra.

Duncan Macrae (1905 -1967)

I have recently had some old cine films put onto DVD, one is of them singing at Mum and Dad's Silver wedding meal,

---

[15] http://www.rampantscotland.com/songs/blsongs_sparra.htm

sadly there's no sound, but I can hear them singing in my head and the memory of them still brings a smile.

Games involving dried peas, saucers and straws were part of the fun and very competitive. Teams were chosen and one pile of peas transferred to the next saucer by sucking them up one by one via the straw and transferring to the other saucer. Another game involved straws and polo mints which would be passed from team mate to team mate by hooking on the straw which was held in the mouth. The polo had to be passed without touching the straws. These games were taken very seriously but always ended up with the spectators including, my matriarchal Gran, giggling with laughter. There were a few "cheats" in the family but they shall remain nameless! At wedding receptions these games would also be played and dispersed between the games would be classics such as The Penny Waltz and Knights, Cavaliers & Horsemen. I was often picked quickly for this last one as I was light and easy to lift and throw about!

Aunt Nora

Aunt Nora made clothes for both my sister and me. Bridesmaid dresses and bridal gowns would be produced too for family and others in the village. It has been said she made a pair of shorts for my brother out of one of my Dad's cloth bunnets (cap)! In the fifties they were quite large and so would have had a decent amount of material which could be re-used when bits became worn, but it must have been a fair old size of a bunnet to produce a pair of shorts. She was a tailoress to trade and taught me how to dress make too, supplemented with what I also learned at school. She was our "maiden" Auntie and had a great love for all children. After the war she worked in a children's nursery in Greenock. When I was born the midwife passed me to Aunt Nora she was the first to hold me, even before my Mum. There was one time Aunt Nora carefully set the material on the table and meticulously pinned the pattern on. She then deftly cut around the pattern using her shiny long steel shears with the bright red handles. It was only when she finished that she realised she had also cut the table cloth in the pattern pieces of the dress she was cutting out! Another time, probably after the table cover episode, she laid the material and pattern out on the floor. She again deftly cut around the pieces when suddenly there was a loud bang and a flash and she flew backwards across the room! She had cut through the cable of the standard lamp which was plugged into the main socket, there were no safety trips in those days. Her lovely shiny shears had a large hole in them and that was the last piece of material they ever cut.

The day Aunt Nora passed away will be forever etched on my memory. Mum was still in hospital in Greenock after her stroke and they were looking to discharge her back to the flat where she lived with my Dad. It was not particularly wheelchair accessible. Usually in a situation like that there would have been a home visit planned, but there was no talk of this. After discussion with Mum and the hospital it was agreed she would go home for an afternoon and a wheelchair accessible taxi was organised. Aunt Nora was in hospital in Paisley and was deteriorating health-wise. As I was coming from Fife the staff made an allowance for me to visit out with stipulated visiting times. I arrived at the hospital and Aunt Nora was unconscious. She was presenting with a form of breathing which from my nursing days I knew signalled that the end was very near. Even although unconscious, hearing is the last sense to fail and so I read a Psalm and prayed audibly with her. I didn't want to leave her, my Mum would always have sat with a person, so they were not alone in the last moments of life. In my nursing training this was very strongly emphasised too, but I was torn between wanting to stay and wanting to go and support Mum in her afternoon at home. I spoke with the nurse in charge and she confirmed my thoughts that Aunt Nora's time was short. She encouraged me to go on and be with Mum and assured me that she would have someone sitting with Aunt Nora so she wouldn't be alone.

As I left the hospital I phoned my sister in Italy and shared my concerns of having made the right decision. I travelled on to the hospital at Greenock, arriving just in time. Thankfully the nurses had Mum ready and we spent the afternoon in the flat that Mum and Dad had moved to. I then went back with Mum in time for her to get her tea at the hospital. When I left her I phoned the hospital in Paisley. The nurse who answered the phone was the one I had spoken with earlier. With trepidation I asked how Miss Miller was. She replied, "Are you her niece who was in earlier?" and I confirmed I was. She then went on to say, "In all my years of nursing I have never experienced what happened today. You hadn't turned the corner at the bottom of the corridor when your Aunt's breathing returned to normal. That just doesn't happen! She's very comfortable and don't be concerned."

I went back to the flat and had tea with Dad and we travelled back to see Mum. I explained to Mum that I wouldn't stay long with her, I was going to Paisley and I would sit with Aunt Nora for as long as it took. She was upset. This was her big sister, had she been able she would have done it herself. When I arrived at the hospital, my niece was sitting with Aunt Nora. Within fifteen minutes of my arrival her breathing returned to what it had been earlier. She suddenly deteriorated and my niece went to alert the nursing staff. Just shortly after that Aunt Nora passed away in my arms. The moment was poignant as she had been the first to hold me when I was born and I had the privilege of holding her when she passed away. The Bible describes death for those who have put their faith and trust in God as "falling asleep". The moment of her last breath she was present with her Lord and I look forward to the day when we will be reunited again.

Why am I so passionate about Inclusion?

Family, friends, life-experiences and the guiding hand of God have all had an impact on our decision to build the Rings. Little by little, the idea has grown and been shaped by those we know and what others have told us. Continuing with the family theme, two cousins in particular have played an important part in this journey.

Cousins

My cousin Alex Machray was a twin. Alex and Joe weren't identical in fact they didn't even look like brothers one had dark straight hair and the other auburn curls taking after opposite sides of their family, don't you just love genetics? They were close in age to my brother, and as boys they played together. Often cousins would come and stay at the bungalow in Milton-Of-Campsie and Joe and Alex were no exception, bonds were forged that will last for eternity. Both the Miller and Machray families were musical and we were encouraged to use our gifts. Alex had a wonderful rich voice and sang in a Church group called The Kingsway Singers as well as the choir. He was a soloist too. His gift of singing brought much blessing and joy to many. He sadly developed Inclusion-Body Myositis (IBM) and became increasingly debilitated and disabled due to his illness.

Alex and his family enjoyed holidays, often abroad. When David and I were married we couldn't afford a honeymoon so we had a belated honeymoon to Italy and Austria a few years later, before Ruth came along. Neither of us had been abroad much and I took great comfort when I discovered that "My big cousin" Alex and his family were staying in a hotel (a much nicer one than ours) just along the road in the same town, Lido di Jesolo. Now we didn't spend any time together but I knew he was there and felt safe, in hindsight, clearly I didn't yet think David could be trusted to look after me!

It touched a nerve with me that with his disabilities Alex found it difficult to have holidays with his family and as his illness took hold he would go into a hospice for respite, family holidays were no longer possible without suitable accommodation to go to. I can remember thinking, "There must be a better solution". I didn't realise that the Accessible Tourism seed had been sown.

My cousin Robert, on the Miller side, is also older than me. He was brain damaged after receiving a bad batch of whooping cough vaccine. I have only recently discovered that he was one of only a few survivors of that particular batch. He could be mistaken for being severely autistic as these are the traits he displays. He has mostly unspoken communication, with only a couple of words in his vocabulary but even as a child I could see he clearly enjoyed the parties as much as I did. He would stand beside me and pick off imaginary bits of fluff and give me a wee brush down with his hand. I'm pretty sure this was as close to a wee cuddle as I'm ever going to get but that is fine as I don't like cuddles; perhaps that is my wee bit of Autism Spectrum Disorder showing!

Robert's Mum, my Aunt Bell, was widowed in 1962 so I have no memory of Uncle Jack, although I have seen pictures. As one of my Mum's older brothers and one who my Dad was particularly fond of, it was a shock and a blow when he passed away. Aunt Bell was left with daughter Helen, and sons Jim, Jack and Robert. Helen and her husband Jim had emigrated to Australia and Aunt Bell decided to take the rest of the family to Australia too. Many people in the late fifties and early sixties emigrated with government schemes which offered passage at a reduced rate to encourage workers to move to Australia. Mum and Dad were entrusted with the care of their pet dog, Tweed. Tweed was a big part of my early life, often being my main playmate, I was heartbroken when shortly after we moved to Cambuslang he had to be put down as he had a tumour. It was the kindest end for Tweed but I certainly didn't think that at the time. A number of years later Aunt Bell came back from Australia with Robert and Jack leaving Jim and his Australian wife Helen, along with her daughter Helen and family. They are still in Australia today. These were the cousins who we loved to come back so we could have a party!

I had been brought up in an "inclusive" family before the word became associated with equality and accessibility.

Margaret Clydesdale Machray (née Miller)

My Mum had a severe stroke in 2005 and latterly came to stay at Ring Farm with us. She required full body hoisting, just as cousin Alex did, and again the thought came back about holidays and how could you manage with a relative who has accessible issues? When we were caring for Mum I didn't know where to start to look for accommodation for a holiday and to take her away without any support from carers who came morning and night was quite challenging. These considerations came even before you thought about how to transport the hoist to your holiday destination. A small removal van may be required for the trip to transport all the equipment you would need. Sadly that problem was not resolved before Mum passed away. The "seedling" of Accessible Tourism started to grow into a fragile wee "plant".

I have since heard of people who have had to take a week's holiday to research and try to book suitable holiday accommodation for their loved one who has a disability. It was our friend Mairi who highlighted, "they aren't always accessible even if it says they are." To arrive at a destination which doesn't meet your basic requirements for mobility or personal care is unthinkable for most of us. But for families where disability is a factor, this can often be the case.

Mum always enjoyed her holidays although it was sometimes traumatic to get away. I was often enlisted as the emissary to venture along and knock the door of the bathroom where Dad would be relaxing in a bath. "Mum wants to know," I would call, "should we pack our bags? Are we going on holiday?" The excitement of looking forward to going on holiday and telling friends at school where we were going was lost.

If there was water, Mum had to get her feet in for a paddle. Wherever we went if there was a beach her shoes and socks would be off and her face would light up at the feel of sand under her feet. I remember pushing her in her wheelchair, along Leven Promenade after her stroke. "Oh," she sighed, "If I could only get my feet in for a paddle!" I spotted some firemen checking the water hydrants nearby. "Shall I ask them to lift you down, Mum?" I joked. We had a good giggle. Even after her stroke, her wonderful sense of humour remained. She loved nothing better than exchanging jokes and nonsense with her grandsons. I'm sure it reminded her of her youth with big five brothers.

My first holiday memory was of a caravan. I think it was pitched near Buckie in the north of Scotland. Andrew and Eleanor had been left to look after me. There was a large hill. All I remember was coming down the hill on my bottom. All three of us were covered in mud. My lasting impression was the total humiliation of being striped to my birthday suit in the public washrooms and scrubbed to within an inch of my life! All the while my Mum was giving Andrew and Eleanor a tongue-lashing. Holidays and memories, whether good or bad, are intrinsically linked in my opinion, and even many of the bad memories are good given enough time and a sense of humour.

Friends

Mairi Galbraith and her twin Julie were in the same church as I attended when I was growing up in Gourock. We had a Christian teacher in our first year at school and he encouraged us to sing together, taking us to sing to churches and groups of elderly people. We would later invite Heather, another pupil, to join us and we became a quartet. Heather could play guitar and so we were more independent and could take "gigs" on our own. We were called "One Way" and we took "Oh there's only one way to heaven brother and you better get on that road," as our theme hymn. It was very "seventies" and quite Country and Western style.

Both Mairi and Julie trained as nurses as I had, and when my daughter got married, Mairi and her husband came and cared for Mum bringing her from the hospital to my daughter's wedding and ensured that her every need was met. Mum had confidence in them as they had experience with other family members who were wheelchair users. When Mum was eventually discharged to Ring Farm, it was Mairi who came on holiday to the farm to enable us to go away for a short break. She supported my sister, who came from her home in Italy, and my secretary, Amanda, who had picked up the mantle of caring for Mum and treated her as if she were her own Gran.

Chapter 6: Taking Tourism More Seriously

Let the plant take root

For many years we have had two holiday caravans on the farm. I had some success with them during the peak season, but was quiet at other times. After a break from the eggs I started to advertise the caravans on line and the bookings increased. But I was painfully aware that they were not accessible and to make them so would be cost prohibitive.

After Mum was called home to be with her Lord, there was a time for reflection and thought. The caravans were doing better with our advertising on the World Wide Web. I had a lady phoned me from Falkirk asking if she should come and look at our caravan to see if it would be suitable to bring her son who was a wheelchair user. It wasn't, the niggling came again and the Accessible Tourism "plant" got a wee watering.

I wondered if we could build a cottage with two bedrooms, one which would be wheelchair accessible and with my nursing background I could add a bolt on package of care to assist a relaxing holiday. I shared my thoughts with Mairi, whose brothers-in-law both had Muscular Dystrophy and were both wheelchair users. She said it was a huge problem to find suitable accommodation for holidays. She encouraged me to consider having two wheel chair accessible bedrooms as there were a lot of inherited diseases which often meant more than one in the family or group needed accessible facilities. The cottage would need to have three bedrooms at least. Mairi's words, "Make sure it does what it says on the tin." She meant that it would be truly accessible and not just pay lip service to it. These words have been my "benchmark" and what we are working to achieve at The Rings. She encouraged me, from her personal experiences, to believe that there would be individuals and families who would be looking for this type of house.

SRDP Grant

Then, I heard about the Scottish Rural Development Programmes (SRDP). There were different categories in which you could apply for grant assistance, one of them being Farm Diversification into tourism. The grant is still available but the categories have changed. Applications were based on a points system and so with an application deadline just around the corner and no guarantee that there would be another opportunity, I researched what I thought it would cost to build, we started to investigate getting planning permission and engaged the help of SAC advisors (Scottish Agricultural College) to help submit the application on-line as that task in itself would test the most able of "techy" folk.

A Statement of Intent had to be written and then expanded to include how you would achieve the project you had in mind. A business plan was required as well as collaboration with other businesses. The latter was impossible as what we were doing was so difficult to find and really quite unique, however we managed to find another business that we could collaborate with although it was a very tenuous link and nothing to do with Accessible accommodation! A letter from the Bank was required to say they would give financial backing, to get this letter was another story.

The grant would be fifty per cent of our project cost so would make what we were doing within the financial reach of a small farm. One of the points would be to ensure the ongoing viability of the farm. Owning only ninety acres we couldn't support an income for even one partner of the business. We scored an extra point on the grant scoring system because we'd had to give up the hens after the regulations about cages had been changed by the EU. We had to gather support to ensure that our project was needed. This again opened my eyes to the great need for suitable accommodation. We were able also to state that Planning in Principle had been applied for.

Several years before, we had inquired about planning, with the view of selling a building plot to release funds to re-invest in the farm. At that time one of the local Council Planners came for a site meeting and suggested an area of our land, between two long established independent cottages, as the most likely area for which planning would be approved. He added that had the derelict steading just round the corner been habitable then this little cluster of houses would be classed as a hamlet and would give a stronger case for planning approval. The site has a fantastic view over rolling countryside however we decided that the cost involved for an application with no guarantee of success was too great. We decided to shelf that plan.

In the period between our initial inquiry about planning and our Accessible Tourism plans the derelict steading attracted several prospective buyers, there was a rumour that Sean Connery was among them, which really would have put Chance Inn on the map! It was finally purchased by a developer, David Kerridge and his wife, who renovated the main farmhouse for their own family and also converted two barns for houses making three dwelling houses built to a very high standard and typical of Fife architecture with varying roof heights.

We felt confident that planning would be possible after this re-development and including the two cottages either side of our site. Not to be complacent as any new building in the countryside can be fraught with problems we engaged a company who were Architects and Town Planning Consultants. They started the application for Planning in Principle and suggested we apply for a three and five bedroom semi-detached building. Now, not a huge amount of thought was put into this. I had started some market research, but with virtually no accessible tourism to glean information from and none that I knew of, I had to look at the mainstream market. I was able to conclude that larger properties that could accommodate up to ten guests had good occupancy rates. I'm ashamed to admit that we were not fully confident that the accessible market would give us the revenue required to repay the loans we would be taking, we needed to give the bank some reassurance from a known market.

Our neighbour had approached us looking to rent or purchase part of our field for car parking and we explained that a "Change of Use" would be required through Planning. The timing was ideal as we were about to apply for Outline

Planning Permission and so this could all be dealt with at the same time. Our neighbour left and seemed quite happy with the plan. The consultants took an off the shelf building and popped the image on the plan submitted with the application. Planning in principle was applied for on the 5th of November 2010. I didn't realise at the time but this was the start of our steep learning curve about the Planning Regulations for Scotland.

Our first attempt at the grant was submitted just a few days later on the 8th of November 2010. It was then a waiting game. The SRDP grant system has to be submitted on line, there are no interviews or possibility to put forward a personal presentation, so it was incredibly challenging for a dyslexic, but we were still hopeful that despite the rush to pull it together we had presented a good case. I was encouraged to play down the Accessible Tourism as it was thought it wouldn't be financially viable and might jeopardise the application.

The Planning in Principle was proceeding in the background and we were more than a little taken aback when the neighbours who had requested land from us for car parking, which we agreed to, then objected to the planning application. The local Community Council had been approached by the objectors and I discovered that our business and Planning Application had been discussed at a meeting without any indication to us that this could or would happen. No attempt was made to hear what our application was for and no check was made to establish the viewpoint of the wider community. They proceeded to make a formal objection. We were advised that an objection from a Community Council held more weight than one from an individual. We had more than 5 objections so our application had to be submitted before The North East Fife Planning Committee. Our Consultant then advised us that we should gather support in letter format as soon as possible because the Councillors would want to be assured that what we were building was needed and would be used.

Our loaves and fishes

On the 8th of February 2011 I attended Fife Tourism Strategy for 2010-2020 conference. Arriving in good time at The Old Course Hotel in St Andrews I felt quite nervous as I walked through the wide doors and into a marbled floor reception area. I was conscious of the many thousands of tourists from every corner of the world who had walked over this floor before me. It was indeed a well-chosen venue to hold this particular conference. After registering I was directed into a large room where tea, coffee and mini bacon rolls were available.

I still find it difficult and awkward to walk into a room full of strangers and start to "network", and this occasion was no different. After a brief chat with a tall gentleman who ran a well-known hotel in another part of Fife, it was clear that he was not that impressed with my project or the concept of Accessible Tourism. As he quickly moved on I was again left feeling like a fish out of water. I made my way to the side to gather my confidence before taking another plunge into the networking pond. I found myself standing next to a lady and we introduced ourselves, she was from Visit Scotland. I explained my project to her. In turn she explained that she was Chris McCoy, Equality & Diversity Manager with Visit

Scotland and that she was also the Project Manager for Accessible Tourism. Chris went on to say that what I was hoping to do was exactly what Visit Scotland and the Scottish Executive were trying to encourage and expand on. I must admit my heart took a wee jump, just consider it, a room of at least one hundred and fifty business people all involved in Tourism and the second person I speak to is the very person who can assist me in my quest. Okay, what would you statisticians make of that? Another "you couldn't make it up" moment.

Chris then named a list of her contacts whom I needed to speak with to get their viewpoint. When I explained about our need for planning support she assured me that she would put me in contact with those who were already working in Accessible Tourism and would be supportive, adding that Visit Scotland could give very solid figures to prove the very great need for the type of accommodation we were hoping to provide. This would be valuable information for the bank too as I had found it impossible to produce figures for Accessible Tourism so my figures were based on regular tourism.

Chris' contacts included, Kenny, who had been in a wheelchair for thirty years after a catastrophic rugby injury. He had been fighting for years to raise awareness for the great need of accessible accommodation. Also, Andy, a fit former naval chap who had also served with the Police, who now had Multiple Sclerosis (MS). Andy had started a business to check for accessibility within tourism and compile a tried and tested list of Accessible Accommodation and visitor destinations. Sadly due to deteriorating health he has had to stop his enterprising business. These two contacts and others would help shape The Rings. We exchanged contact details and went into the conference. That "chance" meeting with Chris would shape the next leg of the journey in a remarkable way.

There is an account in the New Testament of the Bible where a crowd of folk are needing to be fed, they have been listening to Jesus and it is getting late. No late opening supermarkets, not even a wee corner shop. The disciples get into a flap and the question is asked, "How are we going to feed the people? We should send them away." A little boy (who is never named) comes forward with his packed lunch. He had been listening to this Great Teacher and I'm sure he thought he was offering to share his lunch with Jesus. The wee boy didn't realise that Jesus was God himself. God took that small willing offering and fed over five thousand men and there were also women and children on top of that number. We had been willing to try to build a cottage for Accessible Tourism with two bedrooms, we had offered our "two loaves and five small fishes" just like the wee boy in the Bible. God had a much bigger plan.

The 15th of March 2011 found me at the Fife Tourism Conference. It was held at The Old Course Hotel and this time the surroundings were a little more familiar to me. It was titled "Big Opportunities to Grow Your Business". Key speakers included top hoteliers and the then Chairperson for Visit Scotland, there were workshops and a very nice lunch. I think there should be training for novices like me on how to eat, balance plates and glasses, network and hand out business cards without pouring something down your front! I do remember thinking that there was no significant mention of Accessible Tourism which I thought strange given the information I had gleaned.

The first set-back

The next day, 16th March 2011, I received a phone call to say we hadn't been successful in our grant application for the SRDP grant. I was gutted, was the door closing on our new venture before it had really got off the ground? I have a little calendar which gives a Bible verse for every day of the year, I came off the phone and turned to read what the verse was for the day, hoping for some encouragement. I wasn't to be disappointed:

> *"But I'll take the hand of those who don't know*
> *the way, who can't see where they are going.*
> *I'll be a personal guide to them, directing them*
> *through unknown country. I'll be right there to*
> *show them what roads to take, make sure they*
> *don't fall in the ditch. These are the things I'll*
> *be doing for them - sticking with them, not*
> *leaving them for a minute."*[16]

This verse has been very precious and appropriate as you will see as this story unfolds.

Just a few days later on the 24th of March 2011 I received a phone call from Scottish Enterprise saying that my name had been suggested to them as someone who may be interested in a group they were trying to bring together with like-minded businesses involved with Agri-tourism. This may be a word new to your vocabulary but I'm sure you will hear more of it. It is well known in Italy and other European countries.

---

[16] Isaiah 42:16 TM

Planning Permission in Principle – December 2010

Objectors to our application for Planning Permission in Principle (PPP) suggested that we should build at the steading and a site visit was arranged for a planner to see the situation. It was explained to him that although small, we are still a working farm and to have heavy machinery such as tractors in close proximity to guests, in particular those with disabilities especially sensory impairments, would be a Health and Safety nightmare. The Planner went back to the office with no doubt that the farm steading was not a suitable location for the accessible holiday accommodation.

It would be some time later when I realised that there were "Important Dates" linked with planning. You are effectively in a lottery depending on whether your region adheres to these dates laid down in legal statutes. For us, one of the key dates is the "Neighbour Consultation Expiry Date". This date means the difference between a decision for or against planning permission being made by the Planning Department or by a Planning Committee of councillors. Now, to most the word "expiry" is very clear in the English language, for example, if our car road tax or insurance has "expired" we are breaking the law if we continue to drive. If my permitted time to start my building after permission has been given *expired* (usually after three years) and I then started to build, I would be breaking the law. I simply don't understand why, then, when the neighbour consultation expiry date was the 17th of December 2010, and the expiry date passed with only two objections, the decision was not taken "in house". In fact it would be the 24th of January 2011, more than a month after the *expiry* date, before five objections had been submitted. Unbelievably, the sixth objection did not come in until the 31st of January and yet still no decision was taken. I was then told that our application, since it had received "more than" five objections would have to be submitted to a planning committee of local councillors. To qualify for consideration, objections have to be "material objections"[17]. This is something that would be even more relevant later in our planning journey. Perhaps I should call it our planning marathon.

Going to a planning committee involved more cost for us as we then had to pay our consultant to prepare our case for the planning committee. Our Planning consultant advised us that we should gather letters of support and that we should write a personal letter explaining our motives to the Planning Committee. We didn't fully understand the "politics" of this procedure and gathered only a few letters of support. In my naivety I simply couldn't understand why we would not be given permission to build something which was so desperately needed by so many in our society.

There was a significant delay as a Planning Committee is only held once a month. To compound the delay the Scottish Government Elections were held in April which meant no Committee met in April. This pushed our application to the Planning Committee being held on the 11th of May 2011. Remember, our Planning application was made on the 5th of

17
http://www.planningportal.gov.uk/general/faq/faqapplyprocess#Whatarem aterialconsiderations

November 2010, it had taken six months to get to this point. The legislation[18] states that a decision on planning such as ours should take eight weeks (two months).

Planning Committee – May 2011

It was a new experience going to a Planning committee. The North East Fife Planning Committee was held in the County Buildings Cupar, in a beautiful room with large portraits of former notables looking down with a watchful eye over proceedings. Local councillors sat at tables placed in an oval, facing one another and at a top table sat a Chairperson, flanked by a Council Solicitor and Planning advisors. There were note takers and a "techy" person who put up, via PowerPoint, various site views of whatever application was being heard. There was a speaker system and the person speaking pressed the microphone in front of them before speaking, it still wasn't easy to hear which was quite frustrating, especially as there were people coming and going as their applications had been heard or were about to be heard. There is a previously published agenda. Some items are discussed briefly and decisions generally are for approval or denial and votes are asked for to determine the decision. Some didn't even get a vote if there was no opposition to the recommendation made. A case officer from planning presents the application and in my experience it is not necessarily the case officer who actually knows the details of your application, which is unfortunate. The public can sit in on the meeting, but no comments are permitted

---

[18] http://www.legislation.gov.uk/uksi/2015/595/article/34/made#

and the applicant has no opportunity to speak. This can lead to a great deal of frustration as questions are asked by the councillors to which the planner may not readily have the answer. The applicant or representative of the applicant could have given the answer promptly, reducing confusion and the time spent refusing applications or delaying them based on lack of information. Something which would have a great impact on our subsequent appearances in this forum and to be frank would save everyone concerned a great deal of time and anxiety.

After a discussion which lasted longer than the combined total all the previous application discussions, we walked out of our first, very stressful, Planning Committee. We had Permission in Principle, with conditions. The main condition was that we had to have a Section 75 linked to the approved plot. This would mean that we had to have a formal legal attachment to our title deeds to say the area designated with Planning Permission had to be part of the farm and couldn't be sold separately. It also stated that the planning was specifically for a farm diversification into Tourism. That was not a problem as this was what we were trying to achieve, but again this would cost more money as it could only be done by a solicitor and the information then had to be registered with the Land Registry for Scotland.

Planning to Succeed

The Scottish Enterprise invitation I mentioned earlier, was followed up with a face to face interview with a facilitator for the "Planning To Succeed" Group I was being asked to join. Vicky listened to what we were hoping to do and then looked at my first, failed, grant application. She said that the grant application didn't reflect what I had said to her, so I explained that I had been advised that for the grant and the bank I should play down the Accessible Tourism. I think it would be fair to say she was shocked and then angry. "That is your USP!" she said. Now I would have known what she was speaking of had she said, "UFO", but "USP"? I thought that was a delivery company! Oops, that's UPS. As I was trying to work out what a USP was, Vicky must have seen the blank look on my face and explained that a USP was a "Unique Selling Point" and that my POD "Point of Difference" was Accessible Tourism. I would learn that if you didn't have a POD you don't have a USP so your business could only ever compete on price. Here, true to the verse I was given, was someone who had been sent to guide me. Bev would join her and these two ladies in particular would encourage and guide me through some particularly difficult times.

In the beginning I thought I was signing up for a one year course. It was in fact three years. It involved monthly meetings with the others in the group at each other's businesses. When it was your turn to give hospitality you would provide, tea/coffee and a lunch. This was effectively the only cost involved. Had I realised I was making a three year commitment I may not have started and would have missed an amazing training for business.

Now bear in mind I was trained as a nurse and had "fallen" into the egg industry by accident. My sister gave me a crash course in how to keep accounts for VAT and annual accounts for the tax man. As for running a business I did that by instinct and gut feeling and didn't do a particularly good job!

I will never forget the first meeting, held at Cluny Clays by Kirkcaldy, on the 15th of June 2011. About twelve of us all in some way involved in Agriculture and Tourism met at 1pm and had a lovely lunch provided by Cluny Clays. After an ice-breaker, Vicky and Bev introduced how the Planning To Succeed (P2S) and Agri-tourism would be tailored to suit our individual businesses. Now, believe it or not, but I have just found the agenda for that day in my business diary. Looking back, I remember questions being asked and us all going around the room pouring our thoughts on to flip charts. What was most important to us in our businesses on a variety of topics? The section was called "Scoping out our group objectives. Dates, Roles, Content, Methods of Learning, Benchmarking, Case Studies, Examples of best practice." It was an "interactive" session in every sense of the word! Well, I have to say at the end of it my brain ached. The lady I was sitting beside raised concerns that this may be too much for her, after all, she was hoping to retire soon and pass it on to her son. I tried to assure her that I felt the same way and I'm sure we would get into the way of it. Had I bitten off more than I could chew? After this intensive session we then had a tour of Cluny Clays near Kirkcaldy and were told how the business had been built up. I held on to the words that Vicky had given at my one-to-one session, that I *did* have a good business idea and that *they* would help me in re-applying for the grant as well as showing me how to be an effective business person. Do remember the verse, I was given the day we didn't get the grant:

"But I'll take the hand of those who don't know
the way, who can't see where they are going.
I'll be a personal guide to them, directing them
through unknown country. I'll be right there to

*show them what roads to take, make sure they
don't fall in the ditch. These are the things I'll
be doing for them- sticking with them, not
leaving them for a minute."*

I firmly believe God's timing was perfect and these two "facilitators" were going to be used to "take my hand and show me the way to go". Without a doubt they were going to "direct me through unknown country" that of grant applications and the business world.

Shaping the vision

After we got the planning in principle we started to speak to architects, one said that he had designed a nursing home and knew exactly what we wanted. Eh, no! I didn't want it to look like a nursing home. I wanted it to be accessible but to look like a really nice 5 star self-catering accommodation. The facilities should be there but not obvious.

I mentioned that we required a Section 75 as part of the planning in principle approval. This is a legal binding agreement. It had to be established that Ring Farm did belong to us, so our solicitor had to request our Title Deeds be sent to him from the bank which held our mortgage. With only a small amount left on our mortgage to pay we decided to clear that and release the security the bank had over our farm. The idea was that this would make the legal process for the Section 75 a little easier... famous last words! It took months for the bank to find our title deeds. They had lost them, or perhaps I should say "mis-placed" them. It took months of phone calls both by my solicitor and myself, several visits, including to their main mortgage centre. After a great deal of stress they were eventually found, a carrier bag full, so you wouldn't have thought that easy to lose!

We had chosen David Kerridge to design and build the houses and he started to show us various options and designs. He came up with the idea of having it multi-occupancy with flexibility. He had designed it built into the slope of the field so from the roadside it would look like a single level cottage, similar to those on either side of the plot. When you came round to the front of the build you would then see that it had two levels. You could book the upper or lower and there were two studio apartments too. It was great, we were so excited it made perfect sense, the only drawback was that if they were taking the whole property then wheelchair users would have to go outside to come down a slope to get to the ground floor where everyone could eat together. As we couldn't afford a lift as well as the running costs it would incur, it seemed a compromise that we would need to make.

To be sure that the building we were applying for planning permission for "did what it said on the tin" we engaged professional help in the form of "Ruby Slippers" (don't you just love that name) who specialised in interiors. In particular they design kitchens and bathrooms, ensuring that the layout is accessible. Whilst this was an additional expense it was critical to the project that these areas worked and worked well.

We were preparing to re-apply for the grant as we had heard there was another round coming. As you can imagine all this was costing substantial amounts of money, but we were determined to get it right.

I should say, whilst trying to pull all this together we were dealing with several other personal and family difficulties. Life is never easy or straightforward and sometimes it seems that life at Ring Farm has its own brand of crazy! So at the end of November 2011, I found myself at Edinburgh airport with my bag and passport, purchasing a ticket to go with my niece, her two boys and my sister-in-law to Germany. I would spend a week there but perhaps this will be the subject matter for another book as there is certainly enough to fill one.

In December the elderly lady I had been caring for passed away aged ninety-nine years and nine days. The Lord had provided this job, although it was more than that to me, as a source of income to see us through the days and delays to this point. I was realising more and more that there are twists and turns all along His planned pathway.

The end of the year came and 2012 dawned I started to speak to other charity support groups such as Spinal Injuries Scotland, MS Society, Motor Neurone Disease Scotland and Alzheimer's Scotland. Speaking with more people who had varying experiences I was getting a better understanding of what was needed but also realising that with the best intentions in the world it would be impossible for me to meet everyone's needs. I was, however, determined to tick as many "boxes" as I could.

SRDP Grant - Ding! Ding! Round Two

The new round of SRDP grants became available so with the help of the P2S facilitators I started to seriously prepare another grant application. As part of the application they were asking for costings for our project, this involved getting two quotes. Given that what we were building was unique and really needed to be bespoke, getting two quotes was very difficult, in fact, impossible. Sometimes the "hoops" that had to be jumped through were very frustrating. We had to spend a considerable amount of money getting drawings and developing the projects with no guarantee that we would be successful in either the grant application or the planning. Neither David nor I are gambling people, although some would say that farmers must be risk takers and I suppose there is some truth in this, but we were keeping going in the strength of the Scripture verses we had been given.

We spoke to the bank who had given a letter of support for the first grant application and, despite the same funding being requested, they said they were no longer interested, so we had to start again and look for bank funding. Our regular bank had also offered support in principle the first time but had taken so long to get us a letter we had used the other bank whose letter arrived in time. It was the obvious route to approach our current bank for funding. I had been with this same bank since I was born and my Dad had been with them all his business life. The manager from our branch came and listened to our proposals. He made all the right noises and said he would let us know. We waited and waited. I asked at the branch and waited and waited.

Then one day I caught him outside the branch. He said, "Oh, it was on my desk, I thought I had sent it out." We waited again, still nothing, so I had no choice but to go elsewhere. Thankfully the Bank of Scotland recognised the potential in what we were doing and agreed to support us with a letter for the SRDP grant. Despite all our delays and difficulties, the Manager responsible for our account, Andrew McPhail has been incredibly supportive. He understands our vision and has been enthusiastic from the very start, including making suggestions as to how cost savings could be made. Our journey has been peppered with enthusiastic supporters and it has helped to propel us along this stony pathway.

Often I felt like giving up, especially when it came to the figures. After hours of work, we again enlisted the help of Scottish Agricultural Colleges (SAC) to submit the grant. As I was going through the figures with Charlotte from SAC, we were then told that our grant wasn't the full fifty per cent and that this round had been changed and the grant would now be "capped". We had a substantial deficit, we had to go back to the plans and discuss with our designer what we could do to reduce costs. Charlotte informed me that twenty other prospective applicants had dropped out, the hoops were simply too difficult. I must admit I felt the same way but reminded myself of Alex and others who needed a holiday destination like we hoped to provide.

We again looked at floor plans, pulled in our belt and adjusted the figures. We submitted the application, our second attempt to achieve an SRDP grant, on the 22nd February 2012. This was not before one final drama, when the system being used to upload the information crashed and the whole system stalled. I received an email at 3.55pm from Charlotte to say she had successfully uploaded our application, the deadline was 4pm, whew!

At this time we had two wee boys staying with us, again enough subject matter for a book and I was back watching the clock for school runs and homework along with trying to help them deal with the challenges in their family life.

"Are they hooses built yet?"

The 8th of March was my Dad's 92nd birthday, things hadn't been easy over the previous few years as he struggled with age and the problems it brought. I was often in the firing line as he would vent his frustrations. In the last months of his life, however, he was always happy to see me when I visited him in the nursing home. Usually his first words would be, "have you got those hooses built yet?" When I would try to explain the challenges we had and were still facing with planning and grants, his reply would be "I would get them built and get the permission after!" In his day this probably was how it was done, but things are very different now.

On the 9th of March I crashed my car. I wasn't hurt but the car was important, it was a wheelchair accessible car and we had bought it when Mum came to live with us, it had precious memories, but would also have been very useful for some of our prospective guests, particularly if they needed transport from the airport.

Dad came down with Norovirus and was admitted to hospital, he pulled through and was discharged back to the nursing home but never really fully recovered, we visited as much as possible, juggled the wee boys and dealt with the two other big family issues one of which was in Germany. I was juggling a lot of balls in the air, all of them major but in the knowledge that God permits things to happen in life, I depended more heavily on Him to see me though. Dad was called home on the 20th of May 2012, he wasn't to see "the hooses built".

Chapter 7: More than just bricks and mortar

When the little seed of Accessible Tourism had been planted, it hadn't occurred to me that there would be so much to do. A vision is one thing, but applying for the grant, contending with planning regulations and creating a business from it all was becoming more of a jungle than just a little potted plant!

Branding

During the Planning to Succeed course, one of the subjects we looked at in relation to our businesses was "Branding". Now, this is a huge subject and there are specialists in Marketing to whom you could pay large amounts of money to come up with ideas to "Brand" your business. We had no budget for this, and so I had to come up with the brand myself. This kind of creativity was to me, like being faced with a brick wall. I decided that in overcoming obstacles simple is often best. I feel I have reached a stage of life where I don't 'get' half of the TV advertising and the other half would put me off buying the product. So simplicity was going to be my benchmark.

"The Rings" was the original name for our farm which is now called "Ring Farm". We have been told by Fife Council Archaeology Department that our farm is built on a now lost Iron Age Fort. The ring which can be seen from an aerial photograph taken years ago is evidence that an historic circular enclosure was once visible near or on the site, probably dating from about two thousand years ago. When thinking of what to name the accessible holiday accommodation on our farm it seemed to be a simple name to remember and would be easily translated if we were thinking of a global market, which is true of Accessible Tourism.

What about a logo?

Again, with no budget I looked to free logos and couldn't quite believe it when I saw the perfect graphic. Immediately it occurred to me that it could look like rings for your finger or heads and arms of people embracing each other as a family or friends would. It would do the job fine.

Other Planning to Succeed session topics included, Working with Social Media, Managing your Customer Database, Cost Effective Marketing, Online Tools, Managing Yourself and Motivation. I particularly enjoyed the session on Financial Analysis. I lack some confidence with figures because of my Dyscalculia, however this session gave me the confidence to tackle it head on. I began to understand that your business accounts were not something you just received once a year. It was a monthly aspect of your business you should be keeping a close eye on. If you felt there was something in your accounts which didn't reflect your gut feeling for the business it was important to question this because it could be that there's something missing from your accounts. All the sessions were tailored to meet the needs of our individual businesses.

Funding

There was some further exchange of emails as well as phone-calls with our case officer for the grant, the problem was costings. They were asking for a much more detailed breakdown of our figures. This was something I couldn't provide, as we didn't have detailed drawings which would have cost in the region of £8-10,000. Without the detailed drawings we couldn't get the detailed quotes. It was a vicious circle and I made the point that it was unreasonable to expect a small family business to make this size of investment without some guarantee that we had a grant to take the project forward.

I heard nothing more about the grant until after the RPAC committee sat in June 2012. I did however, at the beginning of July, receive an email informing me that whilst the application approvals hadn't been decided the SRDP approved capital works would need to be completed and claimed for in 2013. We would have to have the build completed by the end of 2013 and have all the paperwork satisfactory or the grant, in its entirety, might not be payable! It felt like the carpet was being pulled away from under our feet again. I must admit I was more than a tad frustrated as on our application we had clearly shown that our completion date would be in 2014 and nothing was flagged up at the application stage to indicate that for us this wouldn't be possible. We hadn't even got our planning application in and with the best will in the world these matters take time not to mention the build time. Daunted but not dissuaded we pressed on with the design, we realised we were taking a risk but time was against us.

Interestingly we received a communication asking for permission to use our project for publicity regarding the SRDP grant. I held on to that little thread of hope that they were at least giving our project careful consideration.

In August the country was caught up in Olympic fever but for us it was the Paralympic games which took on a whole new meaning. David in particular was enthralled by them and whilst he had always been supportive of the project the energy of the athletes seemed to spur him on. The boost to our enthusiasm came at just the right time as the journey was going to get longer.

Finally, on the 17th of August 2012, I received a text from David to say that he'd had a call from SAC to say our grant approval was showing on-line. We would later discover it was awarded with conditions which were that planning be approved and that we supply two detailed quotes. We were in a catch-twenty-two situation. We wouldn't have the detailed drawings until we knew if we were getting the grant, but we couldn't get the grant without the detailed drawings! That was fine, and at least our developing the plans hadn't been a waste of money, or so we thought!

Oh, did I mention that over the summer two of our sons became engaged? So into the mix were thrown two weddings, one in January 2013 the other in July 2013, and all the preparations which come with such special occasions. It was lovely to have other more happy things to focus on when the going got tough.

On the 5th of November 2012 I sent an email to Vicky regarding hosting the Planning to Succeed sessions into 2013 "It is only a thought but if the Ring Farm session was slotted in a month or two later, it may be that we could have the session in "The Rings", that is if things go according to plan!" They would go to God's plan but His timing was very different from ours!

Planning application – November 2012

Our planning application was made on the 11th of November 2012 but it would take a further fifteen days before it was validated on the 26th of November; more delays and the clock was ticking. The neighbour consultation **expiry** date was the 22nd of December 2012 and the planner knew that we had a grant with a deadline. We were fairly confident of a positive outcome, having obtained Planning Permission in Principle (PPP). We were hopeful that the hard work had been done, how wrong could we be?

We understood we would be applying for something called Approved Recommended Conditions (ARC), this means that the approval is only related to what the building will look like. It presupposes that approval has been granted for something to be built and focuses on the details of what has been designed. We had been given permission to build a three and a five bedroom one and a half storey house, but our developer had designed two four bedroomed houses one on top of the other. This resulted in it being classed as a new Full Application, despite the fact that it was still one and a half storey and the elevation visible from the road would look like a single storey house. This change in classification for our application opened the door for comments to be received regarding matters which had already been approved under the PPP, such as the fact that we were building in the countryside and the access road. It was as if the Planning Permission in Principle did not exist.

This design was by David Kerridge who had developed the farm steading only a few hundred yards away, the development I spoke of earlier, which had helped to quantify ourselves as an "Hamlet". He had designed our development in keeping with these buildings which had been approved for planning and been built. It soon became clear that the PPP was not worth the paper it was written on. I thought the principle to build had been established but again there were objections which raised all the previous points, such as building in the countryside and the road, even although these matters had been approved in the PPP. I felt these should not have been counted as "Material Objections" as they had already been passed and approved, but they were all counted in. We were told that as we had more than five objections then the decision would have to be taken at a Planning Committee. This would be our second planning committee and would mean a further delay which we could ill afford. Almost all of the objections were focused on the fact that we were building. However this had already been established at the PPP stage. These objections should never have been considered as they were not "material objections". However, the argument from the Council was that this was a new full application and all objections would be considered.

As the objections came in we were able to read them online. Attached to one, was a leaflet that had been distributed in the locality. It was an invitation to villagers to attend the local Community Council, voice their objections and also to submit objections to the planning process. I have no issue with this, what I do have an issue with, is that we were not part of this process. We only discovered after the meeting on the 14th of January 2013 that our business had been discussed in a public forum; we were omitted from the debate.

I had previously challenged the Community Council on this point. They had entered an objection for the PPP after discussing our planning application at one of their public meetings. At no time were we informed of the possibility of discussion. Two or three objectors had attended but the impression given was that a large proportion of villagers objected to our plans, we felt this was completely misleading. I later challenged the Community Council about this. I was told they don't know what will be discussed. Again, I would discover later, that it was on their printed agenda. I doubt anyone would argue that this is far from a transparent process. It was very draconian behaviour and contrary to their own rules which states they have to seek the opinion of the community.

Support for planning

The planning committee was to be heard on the 27th of February 2013 we had several letters of support, many from key groups such as MS society, Spinal Injuries Scotland and Visit Scotland to name but a few. All of these can be viewed online at Fife Planning Simple Search.

Reading through the letters of Objections upset me, as clearly many had been misled as to what we were doing. It was stated we should be building at our farm steading. Had we been given the chance to explain we would have been able to point out that the heavy machinery which we used in and around the farm steading made it unsuitable to site the project there. They were also ignoring the fact that we had PPP and a section 75 already in place and insisted that we could build anywhere on our farm. This was totally untrue and the site for the section 75 is documented and has an attached map clearly showing the boundary of the legally binding area referred to in the paperwork.

Here is an example of one of the letters of support:

"I am saddened that in a day and age where we live for 'equal opportunities' there are those would make objections to a worthy cause like this. As a nurse who works within a community setting, I am involved with the general public every week and see life 'as it really is' for some. Those who struggle to support loved ones with physical disabilities and degenerative conditions and long for somewhere away from the 'four walls' that they call home. Yet for many, a trip away or a holiday is completely out of the question.

(a) They have got too much equipment to take with them or they could not dream of a holiday without a hoist within their living accommodation.
(b) They cannot FIND suitable accommodation within Scotland or those that are there are so popular, there is never a 'slot' available to book for time away.
(c) They lack the confidence to go to a facility that is deemed suitable for disabled people,

but actually lacks everything they need for a holiday with complete peace of mind.

For many, a holiday is only a dream of something they once had; a distant memory of perhaps how life used to be but not something that they could ever contemplate now. For some, they don't even have the 'luxury' of a memory. Mrs Henderson has only to be commended for this project. I cannot tell you how I would feel to be able to say to some of my patients, 'I think I might have found you the perfect getaway.'

As someone who has spent time at Ring Farm, I am fully able to commend this spot as a place of unsurpassed beauty with an abundance of wildlife and general tranquillity. A place that would make for the holiday of a lifetime for someone who has been forbidden this privilege because our society lacks accommodation for them. Please look at this plan through the eyes of someone who can only imagine what it would be to sit at a window and look out to beautiful countryside whilst confident in the knowledge that their physical living conditions are fully suited to make that enjoyment complete. We never know what is ahead of us all, so let's consider those who, through no fault of their own, are unable to fully enjoy all that we can. Let's have the vision that Mrs

Henderson has and commend and not condemn."

Visit Scotland wrote a very supportive letter for the Planning Committee, clearly presenting the Business Case for Accessible Tourism and highlighting that they received many inquiries for Accessible accommodation and had difficulty recommending properties to them. Other support came from my new "contacts". Kenny made some significant points to the councillors in his planning support statement:

"Over the past 30 years, hotel and self-catering facilities have made significant advances on Access issues for All, but on the provision of 'Accommodation for All' - a Scottish Tourist Board flagship statement - the results have been embarrassing and shameful. However, this modest project at Ring Farm can help start putting that right for the county and indeed much of Central Scotland.

Here are three facts that Kenny presented in his letter in support of The Rings to the planning committee:

(1) A 2005/06 report by 'Capability Scotland' found that the Scottish accommodation industry is losing one million beds annually through lack of specialist facilities for the less able. In economic terms alone that is very significant for Fife. In human terms it is hugely frustrating, damaging and the very opposite of equality for all!

(2) Spinal injury is but one of a range of disabilities that result in a person and his/her spouse, carer and family requiring specialist accommodation and on occasion, support

nursing skills for when 'away from own home'
accommodation. Significantly, the Ring Farm
cottage owners bring 30+ years of professional
nursing skills and expertise to clients requiring
specialist accommodation and support – and
as much again in both countryside education
and practical knowledge.

(3) In 2009/10 alone, of the 100+ people
treated for long term, high level, spinal injury
at Scotland's Specialist Spinal Unit in Glasgow,
40% will require specialist accommodation –
both at home and wherever else they wish
to/can stay the night when away from home –
as will their spouse/partner or carer and their
families."

Kenny's strapline is "Not just accessibility but Stayability". Accessibility often refers to a business premises such as a shop, restaurant or tourist attraction. This can refer to venues in the locality. Stayability means that someone can go to another area and be able to stay there in accommodation which meets their needs and access the amenities in that area.

Second Planning Committee – February 2013

The morning of the committee arrived my friend said she would come with me, before I left the house I lifted my Bible and the reading that day was from Psalm 16 as I read it, verse 8 jumped out the page at me:

*"I know the Lord is always with me, I will not
be shaken for He is right beside me"*

I remembered asking God, "Am I going to get bad news today? Am I going to be shaken?" I hurried out the door, as I didn't want to be late. I met my friend and we made our way into County Building where we were met with a wall of people. Our application would be heard on the same day as an application for a major development at a local quarry. It had a great deal of public opposition which was well represented by the public who were there to attend the open meeting. As I tried to make my way up the stairs my way was blocked by an official and I was told that as my planning would be heard in the afternoon I couldn't come in. I asked when I should come back and was told that there would be a phone call from them to tell me when to attend. Having had my business discussed in my absence before, I had an uneasy feeling about this and asked when they usually returned from lunch. I was told in very firm terms that I would not be permitted access until I was called for. He took my phone number and assured me that I would be phoned at least half an hour before my planning would be heard to give me time to travel from the farm to Cupar and park.

My friend had another appointment in the afternoon so had to leave but my daughter said she would come. We had lunch early and waited for the call, it didn't come and Ruth and I decided we would go down anyway and wait outside if need be.

You couldn't make it up, as we drove into the carpark we saw three of our objectors walking to their car. I was shocked and angry as I suspected I had been excluded from the process and my business had been discussed without me. The situation was reminiscent of what had happened with the Community Council. Ruth tried to calm me and said that we should wait to see what had happened. We entered the building and were asked to wait then the same official who had prevented our admission confirmed that our application had been heard and refused but he didn't know the details.

I was "fit to be tied". I was outraged! I challenged him, reminding him what he had told me about being called. He simply said that he had passed the information on; it was someone else's fault. "Isn't it always?!" I thought. I was told that it didn't matter as I couldn't have said anything anyway. That was not the point! I would have heard the discussion. Ruth and I proceeded up the stairs and quietly entered the chamber, proceedings were drawing to a close and when I was sure the meeting had concluded as everyone began to pack their briefcases, I stood up and addressed all present.

I introduced myself and I told them that I had been refused entry in the morning, I had effectively been excluded from proceedings. I added that we had been abused in this process and that the project was now unlikely to go ahead due to us losing the grant and many less able than those present would be denied the right to have a holiday with their family. Yet again they were being discriminated against through no fault of their own. Surprisingly, later one of the councillors said they were impressed with my calmness and ability to speak firmly and with conviction. That has been a mystery to me as internally I could easily have "lost the plot" and read the riot-act at them! Suddenly the verse I had read that morning flashed back into my mind, remember Psalm

16 verse 8, "I know the Lord is always with me, I will not be shaken for He is right beside me".

The chairperson immediately approached me and called for the legal advisor to try to do something, but the deed was done. There was no route to rescue our plans from this planning committee at least. One of those present was able to tell us that planning permission had been refused, with no discussion. We would later discover that one councillor had objected on grounds of "scale" and no one else had entered the debate. Thus it was refused without even a discussion. All of this was made all the more frustrating as Fife Council Planners, who had required a University qualification and years of experience to make these decisions, had recommended our plans for approval. I couldn't understand why this was overruled by local councillors.

Prior to the planning committee we had taken a gamble and had proceeded to apply for building warrants, costing several thousands of pounds knowing that time was already tight and the grant which had been so difficult to obtain and which had cost us, by now, tens of thousands of pounds, was slipping through our fingers. To complete a build by the end of the year was fast becoming totally impossible. I was sick to the bottom of my stomach, it was difficult to remember that God was still in control and He was permitting this delay but in hindsight I can see His purpose.

The next day, 28th Feb 2013 I attended the Fife Tourism Conference held at Balbirnie Hotel, I spoke with the Provost for Fife and another Councillor, both listened patiently and understood my frustration and assured me they would keep a close eye on my case. They insisted that they thought what we were doing was great and was needed by many. I also happened to speak with another delegate who also had a planning application at the same committee as ours. His wife had been present and had relayed to him that none of the applications heard in the afternoon had been passed. I believe they had a very difficult time in the morning and they seemed to have "had enough".

We had a Facebook Page and Ruth put a notification on that our Planning Application had been refused. A second cousin saw the post and messaged us asking if we knew that he was a Planning Officer in a different region? He asked if I would send him the information and he would look at it.

He came back to us a few days later and confirmed that we had a strong case for an appeal. He believed that the committee hadn't understood how the building would be mostly hidden, certainly from the road. He offered to handle the appeal for us and felt we had a strong case. My spirits were lifted again although there were now serious concerns that we would be unable to complete the build on time.

Third Planning Committee – March 2013

We had to wait a further month until the next Planning Committee on the 27th of March, this would be Planning Committee number three and the beautiful room was starting to look a little less impressive. The purpose was to receive the wording for the application refusal. The wording has to be written by the Planning Officer in collaboration with the legal team. This proved very difficult as the Planning Officer had recommended approval and now they had to change direction and write a report for refusal. It was a quick execution, "refused on grounds of scale".

Our appeal was submitted on the 2nd of April 2013 and again we waited. There was a site visit by the Appeal Officer on the 29th May 2013. It was a glorious day and I had been advised to keep the people present to a minimum and that the appeal officer should not be spoken to unless she first spoke to us. A little like royalty! There was a gathering of objectors who followed her round and bombarded her with questions. She asked my cousin a few pertinent questions which he answered courteously and precisely. We all walked down the road to see the site from both directions. The proposed site was hardly visible from either direction. The irony of this is, there were no cars passed during this time, yet later in her report the road would be deemed dangerous for disabled people. We were very careful to follow the instructions we had been given, and didn't try to influence the appeal officer. I won't bore you with all the details but we felt the site visit went as well as could be expected.

We focused on the next wedding in July. We were at my son, Paul's house which we were helping to prepare for "newlyweds" when my mobile phone went. I can't explain why, but as soon as I answered the phone and my cousin spoke, I knew the appeal had failed.

"Unless the LORD builds the house, They labor in vain."[19]

The condition placed on the EU grant funding was that we were required to complete the build by December 2013. This deadline was now totally impossible. After all the work, the frustrations, the hoops which we had jumped through and the money we had spent, we were going to lose the grant anyway. I was bewildered, I felt there had been so many "God-incidences", verses of reassurance and voices of encouragement. The question still loomed large, "was God shutting the door, or should we keep fighting?"

If there is one lesson I have learned as a Christian, it is that if you move forward and it is not in God's will then you can get into a real mess! This was a major step at our age and the very last thing I wanted to do was to be going forward in my own strength. I prayed that if God was closing the door then we would accept it but if not He needed to make it very clear to us. David asked me the next morning if I had read the verse for the day. I hadn't, but when he told me it was Galatians chapter 6 verse 8, "Let us not become weary in doing good", we both felt we were being told to keep going. God wasn't closing the door on this project, at least not yet.

The same day I received a phone call from an Occupational Therapist who worked in a nursing home in Central Scotland. He had been given our business card and wanted to book two ladies in as soon as possible. They had MS and were quite young to be in a nursing home. Both were sinking

[19] Psalm 127:1 NASB

into a deep depression, they needed a holiday and the only thing he could offer was an exchange with another nursing home. "Not what I would call a holiday," he added. I broke down as I explained that we weren't built and couldn't get through planning. He was stunned and then outraged, "do these people not know how desperate the situation is? It's all right for able bodied folk, they can go anywhere on holiday!"

When we read the report of the failed planning appeal, there were several things which were wrong and very discriminatory and demeaning to those with disabilities. The question then arose as to whether we should take the next stage and make a legal challenge.

David and I attended a breakfast launch of Accessible Tourism in Glasgow on the first of August 2013. This was an event organised by Visit Scotland and attended and addressed by Fergus Ewing, Scottish Minister for Business Energy and Tourism, the aim was to promote Accessible Tourism. We were personally introduced to Mr Ewing and he was aware of our difficulties. He suggested we think about a re-design and take it to planning again. He added, "Fight for your grant."

Chapter 8: Re-group and Re-Design

Just at that time, Jack, a fellow Christian in our church, handed me a Motability magazine and suggested there was an article in it that might interest us. It was about an architect couple who had built an accessible home for their own family needs, they had two daughters, the younger of the two, Greta, was a wheelchair user. Their house was called The Ramp House, essentially it is a house built around a ramp which meant that every part was accessible by the whole family.

I emailed them and firstly asked them to comment on our existing plans and the failed appeal. They saw what we were trying to achieve and also validated that there was a great need for what we hoped to build. They offered to redesign for us, gave us a fixed figure and said that they were willing to share the financial risk with us and only charge fifty per cent until they had successfully negotiated us through the planning process. A very generous offer, which we said we couldn't accept unless the SRDP grant was still on the table. God was taking us by the hand and leading us. I set about sending emails to everyone I thought might be interested or have some leverage with the SRDP Grant process. I won't name them here but let's just say I went to "the top". This was a lesson I learned when fighting in the Egg Industry.

"I gave you land you had not worked on."[20]

Around this time we received a letter from a Perth Solicitor's office. Another "You couldn't make it up moment" was about to emerge. The letter stated that our neighbour, who incidentally, had vehemently objected to our Planning Applications, had herself been successful in obtaining Planning Approval for a barn conversion. I was shocked, we were her neighbours, we shared boundaries on three sides and we hadn't received a neighbour notification, how could that be? The letter continued to explain that Planning Permission had been obtained and the property had subsequently been sold with Planning permission. A land search had then been carried out as part of the purchase process. It revealed that the boundaries had been in the wrong place for as long as anyone could remember. Half an acre of the ground on which Planning Permission had been given; land which had subsequently been sold, was actually on our Title Deeds!

We were astonished! God had kept half an acre of our land "hidden" from us in full view for over twenty-four years for just the right time when we needed it. The request was made, would we sell the half acre to our neighbour to allow the sale of the property to proceed? Selling the land would give us the money we needed to re-design and pay our new architects. We suggested that a land valuation be obtained, then we could discuss a sale price. The valuation was never done. I suspect because this was no longer agricultural ground but development ground with a significantly higher value. An offer was put on the table and it was nothing short

[20] Joshua 24:13 NLT

of an insult, we refused it and left it at that. A further communication was received stating that if we didn't accept the offer then the fence would be moved. That was fine by us but we had lost profit from half an acre of our ground for twenty-four years and our solicitor pointed this out to our neighbour's solicitor.

I was getting the house ready for Miriam a girl from Spain who was coming to stay for a couple of weeks. It is at times like this that I make a serious attempt to get my "corners done". This was Mum's expression to describe giving the house a thorough clean.

Many years before, when the children were quite small, I had been rushing to get to Kirkcaldy. I loaded them all in the car and headed off. It wasn't until I returned that I discovered that I had not only left the house door unlocked but it was also lying wide open! As I entered the house I could hear strange noises, fearing we had an intruder I lifted one of the shepherd's crooks which sat in the back hallway. I cautiously made my way to the dining area where there was a shuffling noise. There sitting perched like ladies having afternoon tea were my wee bantam hens I spoke of earlier. They were not that ladylike though as they had left their "calling cards" all over the place. The children and I formed a line of defence and they were "shoo'd" back into the farm yard. Now, I won't confess how much later it was, but I was cleaning my "corners" and was sprucing up the spare bedroom when there in the corner I found a lovely shiny white egg! The lady callers had made their way through the whole house, up the stairs, and found a cosy corner to lay an egg. It brought a whole new meaning to "breakfast in bed".

Thankfully when I was cleaning the corners in anticipation of Miriam's arrival no such surprises were found. Mum was very good when the children were small, when she came to visit she would always attempt to "get into my corners". It was always very much appreciated.

Miriam arrived safely, the reason for her visit was to improve her English. This was quite funny as my husband takes great delight in using Scottish dialect when speaking to those from other countries. Miriam's English may or may not have improved but she did learn some Scots! She took it all in good part and very quickly became part of the family. David's sister and her husband had come for a wee break in one of the holiday caravans and we were getting lunch ready when the post arrived. I opened the letters and slumped into the chair in complete disbelief. The letter was from the SRDP. They were making an offer. If we could guarantee bank funding was still in place and give them a time scale of when we thought we could get through planning, as well as a timescale for completion of the project, they recognised it could be 2015 before completion. The SRDP grant was still on the table. The date was now the 23rd of August 2013.

We were elated that the door was opening again. We had lunch and were clearing the table when we heard a car draw into the yard. It was our prospective new neighbours and they looked fraught. We invited them in and took them through to our lounge, our granddaughters call it the "music room". There are two pianos, violins, piano accordions, trumpets, recorders, not forgetting the "moothies"[21] so their description of the room would be an accurate one. The

---

[21] Scottish word for harmonica

couple asked if we knew what was happening with regards to the sale of the ground. They needed to know if their sale was likely to go through. Without the extra half acre of ground the planning was not valid and the property would no longer meet their requirements. We explained that we were negotiating with our neighbour through our solicitors. We were happy to have a quick resolution but could not be expected to simply give the land away, we had after all had to pay for it and not had any benefit from it. They left with an assurance from us that we would do all we could to bring the negotiations to a conclusion. David and I decided to ask for the amount of money we needed for the new Architects to re-design. We called our solicitor and instructed him to make the offer, the ground was worth probably three times our offer but we felt that we would ask for what we needed and let God deal with the rest.

At 5pm the same day, I received a phone call from our solicitor to say that the offer had been accepted. Our new neighbours would be able to proceed with the sale and our old neighbour had effectively paid for the redesign of The Rings. We quickly called Ian and Thea our architects and on the 29th of August we had a meeting with them. Prior to this we had sent yet another email which comprised of a "wish list".

They brought to the meeting details of how their thoughts had developed and had various preliminary drawings and designs. They had also looked at great detail to the Planning Permission in Principle to ensure that what they designed would meet the exacting limits of having the planning considered under an ARC (Approved Recommended Conditions).

At the beginning of September our architects were winners in one of the categories of the "Saltire Housing award for Architecture". The next meeting we had with them was held at "The Ramp House" in Edinburgh and further design matters were discussed. As the meeting drew to a close Ian asked whether we heading for home or "making a day of it". I thought we might pop into Ikea or Costco, but then David announced that we might go and look at a pup for sale! Now, this was the first mention of going to look at a pup and I nearly fell off the chair. Misty our old sheepdog was getting on in years and had developed cancer for which she'd had surgery. We had been told it would return. Since the anaesthetic she had become decidedly deaf. Now, a deaf sheepdog can be a major liability, unheard canine commands can cause chaos!

We drove to the farm where the pups were for sale which wasn't far from Edinburgh Airport. David watched the wee pups run back and forward, some crouching in the ground then creeping forward. One was chosen for its "good eye" that is to say that even at this very young age it was looking at a sheep and had its beady eye on it. That day we went to see about getting a building designed and came home with a pup. No blankets or bedding of any sort had been taken in preparation so this wee bundle of cuteness sat in the foot-well of the car at my feet glancing up at me with great big eyes.

On our way home we stopped in at my daughter and her husband's house to let our two granddaughters see the new addition to the family. "What is she going to be called?" they wondered. Now, working collie dogs all have short names with firm sounds, "Jess," I replied and no one disagreed. In my opinion, she looked like a Jess! It would be a few months after her arrival at Ring Farm before she would start her apprenticeship and unfortunately for me, we weren't far enough into her training before lambing came upon us.

Trying to keep sheep in as lambing approached became increasingly difficult and with one deaf collie and a pup not fully trained, one ends up doing more running than the dogs! Friends were asking what diet I was on. "The sheep diet," I would reply evoking quizzical looks. "It's a diet where you run after the sheep because you can't work the dogs. All these years later and I still hadn't made much progress in my shepherding skills. Fortunately, this time I didn't have to hang Paul on a fencepost and sit Ruth on the fank.

Public Meeting

The suggestion was then made to hold a Public Meeting. Chambers-McMillan themselves had held one when they were building their own "Ramp House". It gave local people the opportunity to voice their concerns, have them addressed on an open forum, and also give others the opportunity to show support

We set about making preparations for a public meeting. Our nearest village hall is Craigrothie Village Hall. It is very accessible so it was a sensible choice especially as we knew that The Rambling Roses - And a Thorn wanted to attend. This was a group of mostly wheelchair ramblers who had become real stalwarts at encouraging us to keep going. The "thorn" is Andy another contact I was introduced to by Chris.

We decided to produce a brochure which would tell the story of the journey that had led us to want to build the houses and give some information about disability and the need for accommodation. My son-in-law produced a high quality brochure and it was lovely to hand it to people. Again many hours of work and preparation with Ruth proof reading all of what was written.

We wanted it to be a professional event so again a great deal of thought went into the preparations and a programme was drawn up. The architects would present their path to the new design. We had worked our way toward this very quickly because time was moving on. I would have a PowerPoint presentation and it was whilst preparing for this that I had to sit down and analyse why I was so passionate about what we were doing. Visit Scotland would present The Business Case for Accessible Tourism and finally there would be an opportunity for questions.

I felt it important to hand deliver an invitation for the public meeting to all the houses in Chance Inn and if possible give a personal invitation, especially to those who had objected to our previous planning application. Many of the objectors didn't live in the locality and so I had to don my detective's hat to find phone numbers and personally invite them to the meeting. In this age of technology it wasn't too difficult.

I was keen to ensure that it was very clear that our purpose in building was to provide accessible holidays and there was no ulterior motive, as we felt had been suggested in some of the objections. I had one-to-one conversations with as many as I could. It was enlightening, albeit very sad, when one responded, "I can't understand why someone in a wheelchair would want to come to your farm for a holiday?

They can't do anything." It is not often that I am speechless, but I was that day. Another said she could understand that our neighbours would not want "riotous children running around". The evening before I received that comment I had been reading about the number of children who are carers for their parents and who help to care for siblings. I was taken by the effect this has on their lives. In response to the lady's comment, I added that I thought these children, perhaps more than most, deserved the opportunity to holiday with their families. She simply hadn't considered that possibility and agreed with me that it had not occurred to her that children were in this position. She didn't attend the public meeting nor did she submit any further objections.

In support Andy commented at that time "It's a bad thing to say but if the people objecting could only experience being disabled, they would soon change their minds". Without a doubt if disability has touched your family or friends you have a very different understanding of disability. I don't mean that you have to have had personal experience to empathise with fellow human beings, but it certainly highlights the challenges that some individuals and families have to face on a daily basis.

I visited local businesses to invite them to come and hear the case for Accessible Tourism. A personal invitation was also given to members of The Community Council and local councillors. It was important we had the public meeting before we re-applied for planning. The 12th of October came, the scones were baked, and preparations were complete including "boards" the architects had made up showing the design process and what we hoped to build. They had also prepared a model which would depict the house in the landscape. I was disappointed that no businesses attended as I felt they were missing a great opportunity.

Only two objectors attended and only one spoke up. The person took great pains to go through details of the failed planning appeal which had nothing to do with the new design. As I said earlier there were many comments in the Appeal Reporter's report that we felt were discriminatory and highlighted how mis-informed some people are of disability. The Rambling Roses left the objector in no doubt that they were incandescent with rage at the attitude of many able bodied people towards their disabilities. One lady reminded the person that despite being a wheelchair user she had recently flown a glider and was more than capable of risk assessing for herself. She did not take kindly to another individual, particularly an able bodied individual, telling her what she was able or unable to do as a wheelchair user.

Some of the objectors had previously informed the Ceres Community Council that the majority of villagers were opposed to our previous planning application, those who supported us from the locality, took the opportunity to make it clear that they were very annoyed that they had been misrepresented. It will be of no surprise when I tell you that no one from the Community Council attended. They were conspicuous by their absence, after all this would have been an ideal opportunity to hear the viewpoint of the community. Those who knew us well were furious that it had been implied that we were only "playing the disabled card". We were well known in the area for being first on the doorstep if there was anyone with a difficulty in need of help.

We drew the meeting to a close as we only had a certain amount of time in the hall. Further dialogue would continue outside. One person said they would rather shoot themselves than be disabled. Had they not seen the amazing Paralympians? What a sad life they must have led to have formed this view of disability. I wanted to encourage this person to read the book "Joni". Joni was left quadriplegic at the age of seventeen after a diving accident. She has gone on to live a very full life as an accomplished author. Her books are well worth reading. She is an artist and composer of hymns which she also performs. She has also had cancer treatment and her marriage survived under many pressures.

One week on we were to have a further meeting with two of the objectors. They still were of the impression that we could build anywhere on the farm and that we were just being awkward. The PPP was on a map and the area with the section 75 is clearly defined and is legally binding, we couldn't just build anywhere. Another comment which had been aired was that if they had won the lottery they would have bought the piece of land. This I think was one of the strangest comments as the ground had never been for sale! There seemed to be an attitude that the ground wasn't really ours and we had no right to make use of it. We made it very clear that the new application would be made sooner rather than later.

Knowing that there was only a meeting of the Community Council every two months I was keen that we should present to them what we had explained at the Public Meeting, so that any concerns could be addressed. They hadn't attended the public meeting and I didn't want to be accused of trying to sneak the planning through under the radar. We were determined to be open and transparent in the process. I emailed the then secretary of the Community Council and was told that planning matters could only be discussed after the application had been made, so I replied asking that it be included in AOB (any other business). No reply was received, so I turned up at the meeting on the 10th of November with the boards we had for the Public Meeting and the model. I was permitted to address the meeting under AOB and gave a mini version of what had been presented at the public meeting, touching on why we were doing it, the business case and how the design had developed. I was received very well with only a few questions raised about trees and landscaping. I left the meeting confident that no one had openly objected.

ARC Planning – November 2013

The ARC (Approved Recommended Conditions) was applied for on the 21st of November 2013, our architects made the submission online and no payment was requested. Now, this was what we expected. We had been told that, having had a failed Planning Appeal, we would be able to re-submit a further application for no charge providing the application was made within the year. This application was. When the application still had not been validated by the 27th November we started to become more than a little agitated. Time was vital, the clock was ticking. We would then hear the frustrating news that it hadn't been validated because it was awaiting payment. We responded by saying that no payment request had been made on submission of the application and we had been told it would be free of charge.

Apparently, only if we had submitted a new full application would we have qualified for no charge. As we were making an ARC application in relation to the PPP, we would have to pay again. I was furious, but couldn't afford the time to fight this injustice or argue the point that no payment was requested. I paid, and the planning was validated on the 28th of November. The clock started ticking again and I would be keeping a very close eye on proceedings as I now realised the importance of the "key and important dates".

The neighbour consultation expiry date was Sunday 22nd December 2013, after this date if there were no more than five objections then the decision could be made under delegated powers by Fife Council Planning Department. At midnight on the 22nd of December 2013 we had NO objections and seventeen letters of support. At last we were breathing a little easier and believed the planning would be determined under delegated powers, no more Planning Committee debates. We were to get a **big** disappointment. Had we been in almost any other area in Scotland that is indeed what would have happened but Fife policy, at that time, was that all "comments" would be taken until the point of the final decision. Yet again, this was going to be a policy which would jeopardise our keeping the SRDP grant. This same policy had prolonged every application we had made.

By the "Latest Advertisement Expiry Date" 27th December 2013 we had only 3 objections and had been   advised that the Planning Report for The Rings would be completed that day. It would emphasise the need for a decision in early January due to our funding situation. Now, bear in mind, we had held a Public Meeting and personally publicised our intention to reapply for planning. The newspaper advertisement had been given its legal time. Anyone would agree that anyone wishing to comment had every opportunity to make their submissions "on time". I trusted that this time an "expiry" date would be just that. Adhering to the intention of the planning legislation when it was introduced. The dates after all had been put into place to "protect the applicant from the planning process being prolonged". I was not being protected.

Then on the 30th of December, I received an email telling me that five objections had been accepted, so we would have to go back to a Planning Committee for the decision. I simply couldn't believe it! Not only that, but the February Planning Committee would be the earliest our application could be heard. I contacted the SRDP grant officer with the news, fully expecting to be told that was it and believing the grant would be lost. I was astounded when I was told "we will hold it till the 5th of February", I breathed a sigh of relief, we still had the grant! Realising that further objections were being accepted we increased our requests for planning support.

"I will go before you and will level the mountains."[22]

Unbeknown to me, a meeting was being held in the Scottish disability forum where different groups were discussing getting young disabled adults away for holidays. Funding was mentioned and it was confirmed that there was funding

[22] Isaiah 45:2 NIV

either through government or charitable sources the problem was the acute lack of accommodation. Then, a lady from Capability Scotland said, "There is a woman in Fife, she is trying to provide accommodation and can't get through planning. I had an email from someone about it. I'll forward it on to you and perhaps we could help with planning support". And help they did. We received planning support from several of those represented around the table that day. You see the hurdles and delays we encountered only highlighted who we were to many who might not have heard of us if we hadn't experienced those difficulties. Our marketing was being done even before the Planning had been approved.

In all, before we went to committee, we had planning support from Scottish Huntington's Association, MS Society, Spinal Injuries Scotland, Chairperson for Disability Fife, The Disability Equality Forum, Lochaber Disability Access Panel, Tourism for All, Ceiling Hoist Users' Club and from others who either were disabled or whose family were affected by disability. It was very humbling and we felt as if a momentum of support was lifting us up and propelling us forward.

One example of the excellent support was from Kenny:-

"On 13 June 2013, on behalf of Spinal Injuries Scotland, I contacted all Visit Scotland Offices in Fife, to help find suitable accommodation for someone with a high level (neck) spinal injury in Fife.
On 14 June 2013, Visit Scotland emailed back to confirm that after speaking to all Visit Scotland colleagues in St Andrews, Dunfermline and Anstruther, that they had to

regrettably conclude and confirm that there was no suitable accommodation anywhere in Fife for people/families with a high level spinal injury and that they were sorry they could not be more helpful.
This new facility at Ring Farm will at long last allow Fife region to offer Accommodation for All to Scotland's disabled community and to overseas visitors"

The Ceres and District Community Council submitted a further objection on the 10th of January. We couldn't understand this, because had they looked at the comments on our planning application they would have been able to look at the addresses and see that there were more local people who supported our application than there were those who objected. They are supposed to represent the views of the community, but this clearly wasn't the case.

We had fifty-six letters of support and twelve letters of objections. The objections were not always "material" and should not have been considered. We had been told this was an ARC and any objections had to relate to *what* we were building not the fact that building was taking place. Permission to build had been approved in the PPP. This is another factor which we feel needs to be addressed to protect applicants.

On the 13th of January a group of us, including local supporters, attended the Ceres and District Community Council meeting, who had already submitted an objection. I had been forewarned that there would be those opposed to our planning application present and I would be asked to address their points. I listened patiently and noted the points made. It was very clear that those who asked questions still hadn't grasped that we were building self-catering holiday accommodation. I was asked, "Where are the staff facilities and offices?" indicating the misconception that we were building a care home or respite centre. Another question was, "What would health and safety have to say about these disabled people using kitchens?" I really couldn't believe what I was hearing!

Despite having patiently listened to the other comments when I was asked to respond, I was haggled, interrupted and felt verbally abused. It went so far that my daughter-in-law had to interject and ask for some order. At that point another attendee also complained about the way I was being spoken to and asked why the meeting was not being called to order. I didn't retaliate and later I was commended for "keeping my cool", again, I didn't feel that cool.

The final straw came when the minutes of the meeting were produced. The minutes stated that there were objectors to the planning at Ring Farm and named them, but there was no mention of the supporters who were present. There was no mention that I had even addressed the meeting, never mind the language and tone of the accusations. It was unbelievable! I proceeded to make a formal complaint to the Community Council and to Fife Council. To the latter I sent copies of all the emails I had received from the then secretary. I was able to prove the point that the process had not been open and transparent.

There were other erroneous suggestions such as the implication that our egg business had failed, which was not the case, we sold the business on. This led to the suggestion that Fife Council should not approve planning as this new project was a Farm Diversification and could fail. It seemed to hold no weight that I had achieved approval for an SRDP grant, remember how difficult that was, and also secured bank funding at a time when banks were particularly nervous about lending. I may be the only business this has ever happened to, but I was asked to present to the Council my business plan for further scrutiny. We confidently handed over our business plan with the assurance that it would not be put in the public forum and would be handled with strict confidentiality. It passed their scrutiny. We successfully jumped through yet another hoop.

"Like cold water to a weary soul is good news from a distant land."[23]

In the midst of these difficulties I drew on times when God had sustained and provided for us in the past. One such occasion was when our nephew, who had been our page boy, went out to Bolivia to work in a school for short-term Christian service. A bit like we did going on GLO teams, only for longer.

During his time in Bolivia, he met and fell in love with a beautiful Bolivian girl named Claudia. A wedding was planned for July 2000. Paul, our oldest son, announced determinedly that he was going to Kenny's wedding. He was not quite fifteen years old and was planning to go alone. He felt justified in this proposition because when he was about eleven years old he had collected eggs in the mornings to earn enough money to pay for his flight to visit his Aunt

[23] Proverbs 25:25 NIV

Eleanor in Italy. Ruth, two years older, went with him. They travelled as unaccompanied minors and were entrusted into the care of the airline stewardesses. No problems were encountered, so Paul couldn't see why traveling to Bolivia should be any different? The fact that Bolivia was much farther away didn't daunt him at all. Paul's determination was known to us and I suggested to David that perhaps they should both go to the wedding. If we watched what we were doing and cut out extras, like fizzy juice, then enough could be saved to pay for flights. A few days later David announced that he didn't want to go without me and I in turn said I couldn't go and leave the two younger ones. When I look back it seems that things in my life have a habit of snowballing!

We decided to pray about it and then asked Kenny what flights we would need to take and whether there would be accommodation if we made the trip. Kenny recommended a travel agent based in London who specialised in South American trips. The journey would involve a flight from Edinburgh to London, then to Miami. From Miami we would travel to La Paz the highest city in the world. A change of flight in La Paz would take us to Cochabamba and a final flight to Trinidad Beni, where Kenny and Claudia were to be married. In total five flights there and five flights back. I prayed that if God meant us all to go to Bolivia then when I phoned to book the flights that they would all be available and I would be sure that God meant us to travel.

Due to other commitments we had a very tight window in which we could travel there and back. I discovered that if we flew in the last week of June then the price of the tickets would be £100 less per person than if we waited a few days and flew at the beginning of July.

I came off the phone having booked six seats on all five flights there and back again on the days that we could travel. I can remember saying, "Well Lord, you will need to provide the money to pay for the tickets!"

That afternoon I made my way to Kinross. The Green Hotel was a central location for Dennis Surgenor and I to meet with the then Chief Egg Inspector for Scotland, Charles Russell. Now, I have no memory of what we were discussing, but as we settled down to start our discussion Dennis said, "Have you heard the good news, Moira? The price of eggs has jumped ten pence a dozen!" I was amazed. The market price for eggs fluctuated but usually only by a few pence. The wholesale market had been quite depressed for some time, so a rise of ten pence per dozen was dramatic. My heart took a leap and I blurted out, "That's because we are going to Bolivia! I just bought the tickets this morning and God is providing the money for us to go." When I got home I began to work out what a ten pence rise would mean based on our current level of production. My figures showed it was providing what we needed to pay the tickets by the time the credit card bill was due to be paid. That week the SEPRA newsletter announced that the price of eggs had jumped because Moira was going to Bolivia! There was much hilarity and Dennis related that quite a few of the producers had commented, "It's a pity Moira hadn't arranged to go to Bolivia a few months ago, we could have done with that higher price sooner!"

When we came back, I was asked to write about our trip for the weekly market report. I think it took five weeks to tell all of our adventure to South America. I wondered about trying to put parts of the story I wrote at that time into this book. Initially, I thought to check back my emails, but then Ruth pointed out that this happened fifteen years ago. At that time I didn't have email, in fact, I couldn't even switch the computer on. So, if any of you are particularly keen to read my five week blog, before that was the fashionable name for it, you will find archived copies of every SEPRA newsletter in the National Museum of Rural Life in East Kilbride.

God's provision didn't stop there, though. As I said, we would travel at the end of June. The wedding was to be on the 15th of July, not being too sure how we would cope in Bolivia we decided to spend the first week of our trip in Florida. I calculated what we would need for accommodation and car hire which would allow us to travel and see as much as possible in our short time. With that figure in my head, I got a phone call from an elderly gentleman from a church in another part of Fife. He asked if our egg delivery van still came to the town he stayed in. I confirmed that we still delivered there and he said he had heard we were going to Bolivia and he wanted to give us something. When my delivery driver returned from his route that day he handed me an envelope. When I opened it, I had to sit down, it was full of cash. I counted it twice, but there was no mistake, my heart could have burst! It was the exact amount of money I had calculated we would need for our accommodation expenses.

There's so much I could tell you about the trip and memories are still very vivid it would fill another book, but I'll share just a few of the highlights.

We took the car hire back to Miami airport, unfortunately en-route to return the car we got lost in the city. Giving in, we eventually stopped and I popped into a corner shop to ask directions. I suddenly realised I was in a dark dingy place surrounded by several bulky men looking very grim and speaking Spanish. My sixth sense kicked in and I thought to myself, "Perhaps this wasn't a very good idea. David is in the car with the kids, and this isn't a good neighbourhood." At that moment, fourteen year old pale and gangly Paul appeared at my side. He took my arm protectively and said, "Dad thinks we should go!" We smiled nervously at everyone, gave them a little wave, calling out "Thank you!" and left. It seems the penny had dropped with David as well!

I climbed back into the car and we drove on. Finally we could see where we needed to be. The car hire place was near but we missed the turn-off. David decided to do a U-turn on this very wide boulevard-style road. As we did so in our giant American style people carrier it was as if we were in a cartoon. David was happily driving along when everyone in the car started to lean to the right hand side and there was a unanimous chorus of gasps. This alerted our driver and he suddenly realised that there was a large lorry heading straight for us as we were heading the wrong way up a one way street!

After all the excitement we took the overnight flight on to La Pas. When we collected our cases one had been totally slashed. There was a Z-shaped scar across the case opening it up like a sardine tin. I had to laugh, the case contained, Kelloggs corn-flakes, tea-bags and other essential provisions in case we couldn't eat the food. We were sitting in the departure lounge waiting for our next flight. Jonathan was becoming more and more distressed. Never one to panic, I said, "Just lie down on the floor and you'll feel better!" What we didn't appreciate was that his asthma was being aggravated by the high altitude and he was suffering from altitude sickness. We were later informed that there is a room provided for travellers where you can be given oxygen to help with these symptoms. I opened my bag to find one of the snack packs of peanuts provided to us on the first flight. The bag is usually wrinkly and easily opened. When I found it the bag was bloated and tough. The air pressure was sucking the packaging out. This was the same as what was happening to our bodies. It was with great relief that we struggled on to the plane destined for Cochabamba and the blue tinge slowly vanished from Jonny's lips in the pressurised cabin.

During one of our flights the pilot announced over the tannoy that we were passing Bolivia's highest mountain, Nevado Sajama. We all looked out the left hand side of the cabin focusing our eyes on the horizon not wanting to miss it. Suddenly the window was filled with mountain and we passed by with the peak almost at the tip of the wing.

When we finally got to our destination Kenny's Mum and Dad, sister and brother had come to meet us at the airport. They had made the journey to South America a week before us. We piled into two taxis and immediately I prayed, "Lord, you'll need to keep us safe here." The taxis were ancient and the windscreen of our vehicle had a large crack from one corner to the other. We found it hilarious that the large gash had been stuck together with sellotape but it was clear that this repair had not taken place recently. The sellotape had gone hard, with a yellow tinge around the edges and was curling up off the stoorie glass. David sat in the front and I could see him looking back and forward as if he were watching a tennis match. Then the penny dropped, at one time this had been a right hand drive car, when the vehicle was imported to Bolivia and left hand drive was required it was easily remedied by moving the steering wheel to the left. However no-one had bothered about the dashboard instruments so they had been left in place. Any brave passenger could keep an eye on the taxi driver's speed, even if the driver himself could not!

Arriving in Bolivia resulted in a bit of culture shock but none of us verbalised it, until a couple of days later when Daniel looked up at me and asked, "When can I go back to my own planet?" The last day we were in Florida we had visited the Kennedy Space centre. Daniel who was just six at the time was well impressed with all he saw. Arriving in what to him was an alien environment was too much to rationalise, he thought he had travelled to another planet rather than another continent!

The contrast between rich and poor was difficult to cope with. I will quickly add though that we have never known such kindness and care as that of the people of the town we came into contact with. There was a wee shop we went and bought our bread and milk from every afternoon. Well, why get up in the middle of the night to bake bread when you can get up at a sensible hour and your customers can buy their fresh bread at lunch time? On the day we were leaving we went in and with hand sign language and making noises like an aeroplane we were able to communicate we were heading for home. The lady came from behind her counter and hugged us as if she were losing her closest family member. We were moved to tears.

We had taken travellers cheques with us but only when we arrived were we told that these would be impossible to cash. We weren't too sure what we would do but as there were ATM machines we thought we would try our Scottish Cashline card. As we stood at the machine, Ruth who was studying Intermediate 2 Spanish at high school attempted to use a Spanish dictionary to translate the note stuck on the front of the machine. As we were peering at the machine we nearly jumped out of our skins when the slot where you would insert your bank card disappeared and a set of eyes appeared! The voice from behind started to speak rapidly in Spanish. Ruth did her best to understand and respond as we all glanced around to see if there was a hidden camera and we were on the Bolivian equivalent of "Candid Camera" or "You've' been Framed". We could hardly contain our giggles as we joked that perhaps the lady was employed to sit behind the machine, waiting for someone to request money so she could slide it out to them. Obviously, this wasn't the case, she was in fact cleaning the machine, but frequently things were not as they seemed in this lovely but very different country.

The week was taken up with preparations for the wedding, these were interspersed with trips to various local areas. One such trip took us into the Amazonian jungle. There were a number of people who had become Christians and the church there was following the pattern in the New Testament to baptise those who commit their lives to following Jesus Christ. While we were waiting for the baptisms to take place in a tributary of the mighty Amazon River, Daniel joined a number of other children who were stripped to their underwear and splashing in the shallow water. One of the visiting American workers remarked about how brave I was. I replied casually, "Oh, do you mean that I am brave for bringing my four children to South America?" She looked bemused and smiled, "no, I mean for allowing your son to play in that water. It's infested with piranha!" I hastily called my youngest son back to my side. He was most displeased to have his fun cut short.

 Not long into our stay unexpectedly cold winds known as "surazos" began to blow changing the temperature dramatically. This was the coldest weather in the area for twenty years. Overnight the vibrant town market stalls went from selling their usual wares to being laden with blankets, hats and gloves. I purchased a lovely cosy hat which is a firm favourite of mine to this day. We were glad to be able to buy something warm as the house we were staying in didn't have any glass in the windows. Usually there was no need for it! For the first time in their lives our three boys shared a room cuddled into the big bed together for warmth without a single fight!

When the day of the wedding came we were thrilled to be present. I will never forget as we all stood and watched Claudia, possibly the most beautiful bride I have ever seen, walk down the aisle of a very concrete school building which had been transformed by hand made decorations. Here we were in the middle of Bolivia and a recording of Highland Cathedral was being played over the sound system. Kenny's face was elated as he fixed his eyes on his beautiful bride.

Two years later David and I returned to South America without the children. This time to Cochabamba, but all the other stories will need to keep for another time as we must return to the planning journey as we faced the battles ahead girded with the promise of God's faithfulness.

Fourth Planning Committee – February 2014

The day for the Planning Committee finally arrived, the 5th of February 2014. Whilst I was relieved it had at last arrived I was also disappointed as it clashed with the residential arranged for our Planning to Succeed group. The rest of the group were on their way to Cameron House Hotel on the side of Loch Lomond to have a two day "peek behind the scenes" with an overnight stay in their luxurious lodges. As the Planning Committee didn't start until 2pm I would miss the whole day but catch up with them for dinner.

There we were back in the County Hall for our fourth Planning Committee. We were unhappy about the very obvious way one of our objectors was speaking to Councillors and to the Chairperson of the meeting before it commenced. Thankfully, I have very low blood pressure so when it is raised it only comes up to others' "normal" level. It was stressful, as again we had to wait until our application came up for debate. At least it was debated this time, unlike the last refused application. Questions were being asked by Councillors about the size of the building compared to the previous failed application. Now, we had been told that this was nothing to do with the failed application, remember we had to pay for the planning application again because it didn't relate to the failed appeal. The planning officer present didn't have the answers to the questions, he hadn't expected this comparison to be made as it was an ARC. Our architect sitting behind us, *did* have the answers to the questions being asked by the councillors, but wasn't permitted to speak. Frustration, frustration, frustration! It was recommended that a decision not be taken until these questions were answered.

We left deflated, still concerned, and by now I was trying to think how I could break this news to the grant officer. I had the contract to sign in the car with me and fully believed I would be handing it in to the Perth Office on my way down to the residential at Cameron House. I think we went for a cuppa and then I plucked up enough courage to make the call. I explained what had happened and voiced my total frustration with the system and how I felt abused by it all. You could have knocked me over with a feather when the voice on the other end said, "sign the paperwork and get it into me as soon as possible." I think the Officer realised that I was up against an unjust system. Yes, it was yet another "you couldn't make it up" moment. He had the signed document in his office in the 45 minutes it took me to drive from Cupar to Perth. I continued my journey to Cameron House, my head was buzzing. When I arrived, the Planning to Succeed ladies couldn't believe that we still didn't have a decision.

The next month was taken up with more emails and phone calls, we needed assurances that the Planner attending the March meeting would be fully prepared and able to answer the concerns of the Councillors. Updates were given to my local MSP who was keeping Fergus Ewing updated as to the progress or rather lack of it and Visit Scotland were also waiting patiently for news.

"Those who hope in the LORD will renew their strength."[24]

The Rambling Roses and a Thorn intimated that they would like to attend the next Planning Committee. The County Hall is on the second floor so I had to inquire about accessibility and was assured there would be no problem.

I had an appointment in the morning at the hairdressers. To make conversation I was asked if I was doing anything special today. It wasn't my usual hairdresser and the girl couldn't believe we were still fighting our way through Planning stating she had read about us "ages ago" in the newspaper. "What's their problem?" a question I'm asked frequently and have been unable to answer.

As I climbed the stairs to the County Hall I was aware of the feeling of having been here too often. I knew, humanly speaking, we had done all we could. I didn't know though, if today would be the day that God would move the project forward or was there something further in His plan which meant it wouldn't be His timing yet? I must confess my memory of this day isn't as clear as some of the others, but I do remember there being more supporters there to "support" us, including the Rambling Roses. The Thorn had intended to come but wasn't so well and had to stay at home.

Again we endured the wait whilst other matters were dealt with. Then, at last, it was 13/03503/ARC "The Rings". This time the questions put to the Planning Officer were

[24] Isaiah 40:31 NIV

answered with confidence and succinctly. One of the Councillors moved to approve the application and a vote was taken. It was almost unanimous with only one objection. There was a spontaneous cheer especially from the Rambling Roses and they were almost evicted from the proceedings, but order was swiftly restored. I took a moment to quietly bow my head and thank the Lord. We waited for an appropriate pause to leave the chamber.

Outside we had difficulty containing our joy. The relief of that moment, after hitting our heads against brick walls and having disappointment after disappointment, was overwhelming. We all made our way to Fisher & Donaldson's bakery at the bottom of the Ceres Road to celebrate. It is bright, airy and very accessible and has cream cakes worthy of such a celebration! Emails were quickly sent to the SRDP grant office and other key people. An announcement was posted on The Rings Facebook page. My phone kept "pinging" as messages of congratulations poured in.

It wasn't until the next morning the reality dawned. We had finally overcome the Planning hurdle, now we had to set about preparing to build!

Chapter 9: "Let us get ready and build."[25]

We spent several months looking at every detail of the internal part of the building, we had to be sure that it would 'do the job' and importantly come in on budget. Our Quantity Surveyor (QS) spoke with different builders and we went out to tender. As before there were delays. This time not planning delays but holidays. However, as we waited, we were making other plans. This time something to mark the start of the build. We had been asked if we were holding an event such as cutting the turf or laying the first brick, the latter would have been difficult as it was going to be a timber kit build with cedar and larch cladding. Our thinking caps went on once again.

At that time Fergus Ewing MSP was Scottish Minister for Energy, Enterprise and Tourism. We were thrilled that he accepted our invitation to cut the turf. Suitable dates were considered and fixed. We looked forward to the 13th of August 2014 with anticipation. Once again we went into plan and organise mode. Invitations were designed, a guest list was drawn up and the invitations sent out to many who had supported us as well as to Visit Scotland. With the invitation was a request to bring a stone, we were going to build a 'Cairn'. A flag was designed and made and most importantly a plaque which the Minister would unveil.

---

[25] Joshua 22:26 NIV

Care went into the wording for the plaque and I was able to find a company who would also write it in Braille. It reads as follows:

13th August 2014

Fergus Ewing Minister for Energy, Enterprise and Tourism and other supporters marked the beginning of the build by bringing stones for this cairn as a lasting reminder of the journey taken by the Henderson family to build "The Rings".

As I ran my fingers over the Braille I was emotional. Finally, at long last, there was something tangible to show for our efforts. It was a long way from a building but it was something physical nonetheless. Now don't jump to the conclusion that I can read Braille I can't but I thought of the day that, God willing, someone will come to The Rings and it will speak to them.

Here is a little of what the guests that day heard as I stood to address the modest crowd:

You, our supporters, were asked to bring stones to build a cairn. But why a cairn? We thought it appropriate to build a cairn to mark this stage of The Journey to The Rings. A cairn is traditionally known in Scotland but also used as a "trail marker" all over the world, it is recognised internationally.

The inspiration came from one of my favourite accounts in the Old Testament which is recorded in Joshua chapter 4. It recounts another journey that was taken, long ago. The Children of Israel were faced with the river

Jordan in front of them. It was a massive barrier to reaching their destination, something which seemed totally impossible, but the waters parted and they walked across on dry ground; God opened up the way.

God told them to take stones from the bed of the dry river and they were to build a cairn. God said, "When your children ask – 'what do these stones mean?' - tell them... 'These stones are to be a memorial' [26]."

This is why we have asked you to bring stones and build a cairn as a memorial. So when people ask, "What do these stones mean?" We will be able to tell them of Our Journey to the Rings. Of the support so many people gave and how God brought the right people across our path, to encourage us and open the way for The Rings to be built.

The Minister will shortly unveil a plaque. The plaque has been attached to a paving slab, a man made stone, which you might think a strange addition to a cairn of stones. However, my Mum and Dad's business for many years was making paving slabs. Their strap line was "Let Machray pave the way." and it was their business success that helped pave our way to Ring Farm.

The plaque is covered by a curtain made of Henderson tartan which is held by a walking stick which belonged to my grandfather, Alexander Brown Machray. My cousin Alex,

---

[26] Joshua 4:6-7 NIV and Joshua 4:21-22 NIV

was named after our grandfather. Alex developed a degenerative illness, it was his difficulty in having family holidays that planted the seed for The Rings. Sadly for us, he passed away a few years ago. Alex remained positive and kept going through his illness. When I felt like giving up I thought of Alex and remembered why there was a need for The Rings. His niece, Yvonne, is here today and has prepared the refreshments we will enjoy later."

I then went on to share the highlights from everything you have been reading so far, "The Journey to the Rings".

"Do your planning and prepare your fields before building your house."[27]

We thought we were just about there and hoped to start building in the October, but there was to be another hurdle. Only four of the eight tenders were returned and they were all very much higher than we could have imagined. We contemplated the prospect of still not building, we certainly couldn't start until we pulled this in to the budget.

Whilst this was going on we were invited to attend the Scottish Parliament to listen to the Accessible Tourism Debate. The chamber was well filled and we listened as introductory speeches were made. The debate commenced and one MSP from the West of Scotland admitted that she didn't know much about Accessible Tourism so had

---

[27] Proverbs 24:27 NLT

'googled' it. There she read of a couple, David and Moira Henderson in Fife – at which point I nearly fell off the chair - who had been struggling to get started to build suitable accommodation. She stated in the Scottish Parliament that we should be commended for our efforts and she hoped more businesses would follow our example. I could have wept as we still didn't know if or when we would finally start. Fergus Ewing also spoke of us and we came out of the building thinking, "This has to happen, so many people need The Rings for a holiday." We had to focus again.

At the beginning of October we held meetings with the two lowest tenders, now they may have been the lower ones but they were still double our budget, so well beyond our reach. We hoped that they would be able to open the door to a price at which we could start the build. Sadly the figures simply didn't stack up. Yet again, it was back to the drawing board. Well, not quite, as we had to stay within the design agreed by planning, but anything we could change without going back to planning had to be scrutinised.

We tried to keep in items that would "future-proof" the building. The biomass boiler had been a concern as companies couldn't guarantee that if we had a breakdown that they would be able to get parts and do repairs quickly. With guests who could be more vulnerable than most, this was a critical point for us. They were saying we would need to have a backup LPG boiler, this would mean more cost and we had to consider how many years it would take to recover our initial investment on a biomass boiler.

We moved from a SIPS build to timber kit. In the time it had taken us to get through planning, building methods had changed and timber kit builds with high levels of insulation were now superseding SIPS (Structurally Insulated Panels). We looked at changing the foundation, every penny saved was vital. Little things became crucial, for example, with eight bathrooms a £50 saving on a sink added up to a saving of £400. This formula multiplied across other items throughout our sizeable build meant that a pound saved here and there could end up as thousands off the total cost.

On the 11th of November 2014 I sent an email to the "build design" team and said, "We have had time to step back and look at this project and to decide if it is possible to progress with it." We asked them if they were able to come for a meeting. Our QS had drawn up a list of builders, ones that perhaps didn't have as many overheads. Around that time my brother mentioned a builder whom he had heard of in our area. My brother lives in Kilsyth but the pastor of his church came from the East Neuk of Fife. A builder he knew had recently finished The Coastline Community Church at Pittenweem, on time and within budget.

I contacted Dougie Bissett by email on the 8th of January 2015 at 20:52 and explained about our project and pointed him to our Facebook page, 'The Rings Fife', it was less than half an hour later, around 21:15, when I received a call from Dougie. He had looked at the plans and clearly had a grasp of what we were doing. He was interested in having a meeting. We were impressed from that first conversation.

I had a face to face meeting and Dougie, we discussed the project further. He said that he didn't take every job which came his way but that his little sister had suffered from Spina bifida and had been a wheelchair user prior to her passing away. His Mum and Dad had been very progressive for their time and had purchased a 'time share' property which they then had converted for accessible holidays. He knew how important The Rings would be and how many families would benefit from holidaying there. He wanted to be part of the build and would very much become part of The Journey to The Rings.

We made as many permitted savings as possible and by February we had a list of builders, including Bissett Design and Build, who had all said they wanted to quote for the work. Now, remember that clock was still ticking. The SRDP grant office had said the last payment they would make would be February 2016.

In the middle of February 2015 we were gifted a septic tank. Now, to many, this would be a very strange gift, and not one to be too excited about, but for us this was another indication of God's provision. It would enable us to cut several thousand pounds off the cost.

On the 6th of March, we sent out tender documents again. We prayed, "Lord we need to know who the builder should be, it needs to be clear, we can't get this wrong." I hoped it would be Dougie. He was passionate about what we were doing and that was important. In the weeks that followed three builders pulled out. On the 7th of April our QS sent us an email. Dougie had submitted his tender. It was very slightly over our budget, but he felt there were still savings which could be made. We just needed to wait until the others returned their tenders. Well, we had a very clear answer from God. We couldn't make any mistakes with this. The one and only builder to return with a tender price was Dougie. Matters progressed quickly after this. Discussions about cost savings moved again, with advice from Dougie. He clarified that some of cost savings we had made were not particularly helpful but identified others which could be made.

The proverbial "straw"

The target date to start building was the beginning of June. This was critical if the final drawdown of the grant was to be made in February 2016. Now matters were progressing too smoothly. We should have expected yet another wee "drama". Whilst the grant had been signed it was still dependent on our final figures being accepted and authorised. Our QS liaised with the SRDP grant office and we came up against a problem. It concerned how we were breaking the figures down, what we were paying and what would be covered by the grant. Then another spanner fell into the works when they said our funding figures didn't add up. I'm not sure what happened but the figures that were held in our file, weren't ours and that was causing confusion. Discussions were ongoing and finally we presented figures and didn't get a negative response. Had they been accepted? We were unsure. We knew we couldn't start without the "green light" about the figures.

Whilst Dougie had said we were starting at the beginning of June I hadn't made it clear enough to him that we couldn't start without the green light. On Friday the 29th of May 2015 I had a phone call from Dougie to say they would start building, a few days later on the 2nd of June. I froze, "We can't start until we get the green light!" Dougie's reply was, "Well if I have to cancel everything that is lined up then I can't guarantee we will get everyone on-board when we need them. I thought, "Right! We need a decision."

I called the SRDP office and was told the gentleman I dealt with was out of the office until Monday the 1st of June. I suggested that the Clerk of Works might be able to help as he had approved the last figures sent by the QS. I was informed they would try to contact him. Shortly after I received a return call to say that the Clerk of Works was out of the office until Tuesday, 2nd June, the day we needed to start. The straw that broke the camel's back fluttered down, hit my back and I cracked! I shouted down the phone, "That is it! I've had it! I have fought this for over five years. I have jumped through so many hoops I'm dizzy. I have been in five planning committees and I can't do this anymore! If I don't get the go ahead today, I'm throwing in the towel but I'm telling you this... *you* can tell Fergus Ewing this isn't happening because I certainly won't!" The unfortunate gentleman who was on the receiving end of this long pent up rant was calm. He reassured me that he knew our case. He knew the difficulties we'd had and whilst he couldn't promise anything he *would* make every effort to try to get an answer for us.

Five o'clock, close of business on Friday 29th May, came and went and no phone call was received. David came home and I related to him the events of the day. His response caused a sharp intake of breath, "Grant or no grant we are starting to build on Tuesday. God will supply the money." Now, it wasn't just the grant money we would be short of as the bank loan was dependent upon the grant. It was *all* our funding.

It was not until six-thirty on the Saturday night when we received a phone-call to say that if our builder was still in a position to start on the 2nd of June we had the green light to go. It was the strangest of feelings. It felt like I had been standing on the edge of the diving board at the swimming pool. I had repeatedly moved back along the board, then forward to stand tentatively on the edge. Without warning, my toes gripped around the edge of the board contemplating the jump, I was pushed from behind and reality hit me sharply when the water hit my face. This was it, *really* it. We were now going to build, it was very scary and exciting all at the same time.

Remember Psalm 56:8, "You keep track of all my sorrows. You have collected all my tears in your bottle. You have recorded each one in your book." That day, there were tears of joy collected in God's bottle for me and recorded in His book. More tears would be added to my bottle and to many others' bottles, when Dougie brought us the news that his precious wife was losing her battle with cancer. The date was the 11th of June, only nine days after Dougie's builders started. We were all in shock and our hearts broke as we thought of the pain the family were going through.

On one of Dougie's site visits I said to him that he should be with Dorothy and that the build must take second place. I was humbled by his response, "I'm here with Dorothy's permission and she is as passionate about building The Rings as I am." What a special woman! Dorothy will be forever remembered in our Journey to The Rings. She was a nurse too and was a compassionate human being who knew just how much The Rings would mean to many individuals and families. Just a little over three weeks from the day Dougie brought us the horrible news about Dorothy's illness, the news came that she had passed away at home in the care of Marie Curie Nurses and her loving supportive family. One of the builders said at that time, "Don't worry Moira, the building will go on. We know what to do and that is the best way we can help Dougie at this time." It was so lovely to see the unity and dedication in that small build team. The physical evidence of their teamwork is the emergence of a beautiful building.

Did I mention "You couldn't make it up"? Well, there's more!

With the planning obtained and the bricks and mortar in good hands, all that was left to consider was the interior of The Rings. I was googling "auctions" and came across a web page "Sweeney Kincaid". They seem to sell off items taken from companies who have gone into liquidation. The process involves online biding and I have to say, it could become addictive. The first sale I bid on was based in Glenrothes, so it wasn't too far for us to go and view what was in the auction. I was at a Visit Scotland Accessible Tourism Steering group meeting on the day of the open viewing, but David and my daughter Ruth had a look. There were some items that I would need for The Rings so I thought I would have a go. After a few days the sale ended and I had successfully purchased five brand new electric knives for £10, two Morphy Richards toasters for £8 each and a box of assorted kettles, including a matching green Morphy Richards kettle for £10. We bought a new baby's buggy complete with rain covers for £6, not really for the house, but a great bargain nonetheless. You never know when something like that could be used by visitors. I couldn't believe it when I picked up the items to see that the kettles and toasters were coloured. I hope they will fit in with the colour theme we are planning as we are calling the rooms after gem stones. The idea behind that is that guests will choose the rooms that they need and build their own "Ring" with the gemstones. Their holiday will provide precious memories that will last just like the gemstones in a ring.

Encouraged by my great bargains, I looked at another sale. This time the items were in Cumbernauld and due to circumstances I simply couldn't make the viewing dates. The lots comprised of various sinks, toilets and the like. Feeling that I couldn't go wrong, I bid for four toilet pans and got them for £3 each! When I went to pick them up I chatted to the chap who was checking the items being uplifted. I explained what we were building and how this bargain would help us greatly. After the auction finished unsold items are moved onto another website which is called "Closed unsold lots". Here it tells you the reserve price and you can bid the reserve or higher. Pleased with the toilets I had purchased, I then bid for a further six at £1.75 each, yes you read it right. It was worth the fuel to go and pick them up.

When I went to collect them I was told that not everything had been sold and there might be an opportunity to speak with the owner of the building. I think he had rented it to a plumbing supplier and they had disappeared leaving him with a building full of stuff which made it unsuitable to rent. One of the employees loading their delivery van gave me a business card. That evening I sent a text message explaining what we were doing and mentioning that if there was anything left, I would be interested in buying it. I added the link to our Facebook page for The Rings. I received a text message back saying that it was mostly sinks and taps left, but he invited me to come and take anything that would be of use as he would like to help with our vision to make it become a reality. He added that he knew how doing anything new took courage and faith and he didn't want any money. Again, I was astonished. Here was a complete stranger offering us what we needed for nothing. Now, that in itself I feel is a "you couldn't make it up moment" but that wasn't the end of the story.

David and I went the next morning with our livestock trailer and lots of blankets to protect our gifts. We spoke to the owner and before long he told us he was a Christian and what church he went to. We reciprocated telling him what church we went to. He asked what had prompted us to think about building accommodation for folk with disabilities, so I explained about my cousin adding that he had lived only a few miles away in Kilsyth. He said that he had come from Kilsyth and that his parents still lived there. I explained that I had quite a lot of relatives still in Kilsyth including my brother and his wife. He didn't know my brother Andrew, but knew of him and his business. When I said my cousin was Alex Machray, he shook his head in amazement and smiled, "Moira, my Mum and Dad are Helen's neighbours. I knew Alex. Fill your trailer, take as much as you can." Now you really couldn't make that up!

I had been looking at different sinks and loved the glass bowl types. They are very stylish and coloured but we never thought we could afford them for The Rings. Sitting there before us were all colours of glass bowl sinks, all still in their boxes. They were stoorie, but "what's a wee puckle o' stoor (dust)?" As David's mum used to say, "God made Adam out of a wee puckle o' stoor!" Some of the sinks came with chrome stands others were the type which would sit on a worktop making them fully accessible. Not only was God providing sinks for nothing but the sinks I thought I'd never be able to afford. As well as sinks, there was a grab rail, new in its box and a shower screen, the kind used while assisting a wheelchair user to shower. It's handy to prevent the assistant having a shower too! There were taps for baths and pop up wastes to name but a few of the other items.

The house that Dougie built

The build started on the 2nd of June and for some time our granddaughters had difficulty in comprehending that there would be a house on the scraped away area of ground. As a hole emerged, Emma aged four at the time, would ask with purpose and great interest, "How's your hole in the ground Gran?" Beth aged six, who loves to make things and see things made, took great note of every detail of what was happening, perhaps she will be a structural engineer, an architect or a project manager having had her interest in such matters kindled. Trenches were dug and what looked like rivers of concrete were poured. The 'brickies' moved in and blocks were laid with incredible speed and accuracy. The unique shape started to emerge and we would have our Sunday afternoon family gathering standing in the middle of this "silhouette" wondering if it would be big enough. Beth and Emma had great fun running along the blocks which would make the foundations, whilst the dogs would run around the outside trying to "measure" the periphery with how quickly they could do one revolution.

Further excitement was the week when a very large hole was prepared to house the septic tank which was gifted many months before. That Sunday the family congregated around and marvelled at the depth of the hole, converting it into a swimming pool was suggested but sadly there was no budget for that, at least not for the time being. Manoeuvring this large bulky and expensive tank took great skill and patience as inch by inch it was lifted from its pride of place position in the field. When it arrived, in February, it had sparked an unannounced visit from inspectors after its arrival had been anonymously reported. We have been reported several times for just about everything imaginable, anyway back to the septic tank. Derek, the digger operator, gingerly lifted the tank from its resting place as though he were moving a valuable piece of art work or sculpture. His digger crawled along the field and up the hill then, as if he was laying a sleeping baby in a crib, he gently placed this very necessary piece of equipment into its prepared home. Checks had to be made at various stages and on one occasion as he leaned over the open tank his mobile phone dropped out of his pocket into its depths. Now, the tank is full of plastic shapes almost like pastry cutters. He could see it lying being held up by the shapes but reaching it would be another challenge. We each rushed for bits of wood to try to recover it and I came back to the farm shed where we had some of the long reaches with a pincer on the end, the sort that folk less able use to reach things. By the time I got back, the phone had vanished from sight, forever to be buried in its own mausoleum on Ring Farm. So if any of our guests should hear ringing in the night-time, don't fear, there are no ghosts at the Rings, it's probably just Derek's wife looking for him! The soil covered over the tank and all that is visible now are two round green inspection hatches. Meters of drainage pipe were also woven in the area in front of the houses. I've been fascinated throughout the build to see all the details which are so necessary and yet, when guests come, no one will even know they are there. So much time and effort all hidden away.

The steel arrived and suddenly the shape of a window appeared, the first vertical part of the houses. As we stood "inside" the house and looked out, the scene was breathtaking. We knew we had a lovely view but seeing it framed in what would eventually hold a window, set the scene in picture that even famous landscape artist Constable would have been proud of.

The walls were made adjacent to the site and were stacked at the side of the field by Deek (another Derek) Stevie, Ian and Coco. Within a matter of days they were erected and secured into position. Like a Phoenix "The Rings" rose out of Gran's "hole in the ground" and with every passing day there were visible changes. The whole structure was wrapped in what looked like tinfoil giving it a space age persona, this of course would be one of the "layers" that would insulate the building and make it a cosy and easily heated home.

Roof Trusses were delivered and put into position resulting in a fuller appreciation of the whole shape. The roof then had to be covered in protective layers in preparation for its very own "blanket". This would be no ordinary roof. Spikes were attached which would later secure the blanket. The view from the roof was spectacular and I remember thinking, "once the scaffolding is removed this incredible vantage point will no longer be accessible." I tried to snatch some moments and cherish this whole process.

The windows and doors arrived on site and I must admit I couldn't bear to watch them coming off the lorry; it was too nerve wracking. These very large and expensive constructed window frames were positioned and within hours we had doors in position and windows closely followed.

It was September, we were only four months into the build and some of the men were working on the roof and others were "cladding" the walls. One part of the house has cedar shingles, they are like cedar "tiles" each one was hand crafted for its own chosen spot, then secured into place with stainless steel nails. This building is a work of art, not only in design but also craftsmanship. It has been built with care, dedication and incredible skill. The other part was later clad with Larch and these beautiful lengths of wood were added with just as much care and attention to detail. The perfume around the house was wonderful, the larch and cedar giving off their own particular scent, sadly this has now faded, at the time it was like a sweet smelling savour rising up to heaven.

A lorry brought rolls of sedum plants, they were carefully off loaded and very quickly were lifted roll by roll onto the roof this time the clock was ticking for another reason. The plants had to be unrolled and the lengths of sedum mat cut to size and laid into place as quickly as possible. The sedum can't be left rolled up for too long or it would die. More men were enlisted to get the job done quickly. The representative from the sedum company, Bauder, came the next day to see how the roof was progressing. He couldn't believe his eyes when he looked and saw that the roof was blanketed in green sedum, he thought it would take at least one and a half days. But not with our special team of guys! It seems the adage is true, "many hands make light work."

The houses had been nestling into the slope of the field but when the sedum roof was fixed into place, the building merged into the countryside in a most mesmerising way. We could hardly take our eyes off it, the optical illusion was impressive.

It would be a few days later, only five months into the build, when the scaffolding was removed and the full beauty of this bespoke purpose designed building would reveal her full magnificence. Appropriately the sun shone down and the blue sky seemed to add a sharpness to the whole picture.

While the sedum was being laid on the roof, inside, the underfloor heating had been laid too. Bright red plastic mouldings very similar to egg trays were placed in position then metre after metre of blue piping was uncoiled and clipped into place. It was very attractive and seemed sad that in a few days it would be covered with screed, a concrete-type mix which came in powder-like form, but it too had to be laid with neck braking speed as it would set within hours. Dougie increased the specification, as he stated that guests in wheelchairs are closer to the floor and less active than most. He pointed out that as hot air rises they would need higher temperatures to be kept warm. To achieve this, the space of the red "egg trays" were closer together and extra metres of blue pipe were installed. The pretty colours would be hidden from view for all who would stay. They will know the effect of it though, as water heated by the air source heat pump will flow through the blue pipes and heat the screed which will act as one large radiator. This is a lovely image of God, He is there, we can't see Him, but we know He is as we can feel the effect of Him.

Interior walls were erected and we could finally get a feel for the size of the rooms and the positioning of en-suites. Excitement began to escalate again. Plasterboard was promptly fixed onto the skeleton walls. I was informed that it was colour-coded. Blue indicated added soundproofing and green was for the "wet" areas such as the en-suites.

Electricians and plumbers arrived to set about their "first fix" of cables and pipes. It was quite a "frantic" experience. There seemed to be bodies everywhere. Electricians were ushered in and introductions were made, directions were given and they dispersed into their various areas of the house working with focus. Plumbers had already started, but they were gathered and introduced. They were briefed and set about their tasks with professionalism. It was a well-oiled machine. Each part was wound up and set off to work like cogs in a fine clock. Each with their own unique part to play in the greater whole.

Just about everyone who had come to the site asked why the road was having to be brought in across the field, this was the route imposed on us by Fife Transportation. There hadn't been any survey but due to perceived speeds and volume of traffic on the Q66 road they stated that the site access would need to be taken from the existing farm road. This was in order to achieve sufficient "visibility splays" for the anticipated speeds.   After thought, discussion and encouragement we decided to bring in a Planning Consultant with support from a transportation consultant. A road survey was conducted over the period of a week. This would establish that the speeds were low and traffic was light. It proved that visibility splays for these speeds would be achievable from the more direct access off the Q66 road.

Planning applications to amend the access road were made. Much to our surprise the application attracted objections. There had been objections to the fact that the road would pass in front of neighbouring properties and now there were objections to the proposal to change this. We found it totally beyond our comprehension. Comments were made to the council objecting to the fact that we would be putting in a biomass boiler, when this changed to an air source heat pump system, there were further complaints. I won't go into all the details as it is not very entertaining, suffice to say, at time of writing we are heading back to our 6th Planning Committee, "You couldn't make it up". I am very pleased to say that the "Neighbour Notification Expiry Dates" are now recognised and when the thirty day consultation period has ended no further comments are received. Fife Council have now come into line with the regulations used in other regions of Scotland.

The decking was added round the house in time for our annual bonfire at the beginning of November. Friends who had heard about our trials and tribulations had the opportunity to view the houses when they came to the bonfire. There was not one who was disappointed and all were very impressed with the speed and quality of the build.

Most recently Ames Tapers plied their trade, providing a blank canvas for the painters. Suddenly the walls had a finished appearance. Derek was back and digging holes again, this time for the LPG gas tank which would be the backup for the air source heat pump ensuring the comfort of our prospective guests. Poor Derek had to dig several holes. The area the house is built on has shallow soil and solid rock beneath. This made it tricky to find a site where hole could be made deep enough for the gas tank! There's a lovely illustration in the Bible about two builders and the different foundations they had. Jesus said:

> *"Anyone who listens to my teaching and follows it is wise, like a person who builds a house on solid rock. Though the rain comes in torrents and the floodwaters rise and the winds beat against that house, it won't collapse because it is built on bedrock. But anyone who hears my teaching and doesn't obey it is foolish, like a person who builds a house on sand. When the rains and floods come and the winds beat against that house, it will collapse with a mighty crash."[28]*

Despite the storms that have raged throughout this project we have a solid foundation and know that God is in control.

It has been lovely to witness the happiness of our fantastic team of workers. The sense of humour is a real boost to morale and a comfortable fit with our own family. We hope this is the beginning of fun in the Rings and that laughter will continue to echo around the houses as holidays and memories are made.

---

[28] Matthew 7:24-27 NASB

Chapter 10: "Call to Me and I will answer you, and I will tell you great and mighty things, which you do not know."[29]

At the beginning I didn't know how or where to start this story and now I don't know where to stop.

Perhaps the reason is that as I write, the houses are not yet complete. I'm sure there are other "You couldn't make it up" stories to come but this book needs to go to print. You need to hear the story.

We are hoping that the sales of this book will help us to buy some of the equipment that has had to be put on hold after our budget was eroded away with the challenges we have encountered. You never know, perhaps that hot tub or hydro therapy pool may again become a reality including a hoist for access of course! If you are ever near us and would like to, we would love for you to bring a stone for our "cairn" because you too are now part of our journey.

God doesn't make any mistakes and if everything had gone smoothly in the very beginning then there wouldn't have been a story to tell. We would have missed out on experiencing all these miracles. Not to mention we would

---

[29] Jeremiah 33:3 NASB

never have encountered the fantastic characters and "helpers" that have been sent our way.

Our difficulties and challenges have also given us just a little glimpse of the discrimination, difficulties and challenges that families face when illness and disability intrudes into their lives. We hope the Rings will be a haven in their lives, a destination in which to relax and revitalise or to use as a base from which to adventure.

Our vision for the Rings is that it will be a place to build memories. We hope our guests will look back on The Rings with a smile on their faces and know how special Ring Farm is. A little bit of God's beautiful world entrusted to The Henderson family for this time of God's grace.

If you would like to follow our progress:

Find us online at **www.therings.co.uk**

Follow us on Facebook at
www.facebook.com/TheRingsFife/

Acknowledgements

There are so many people I need to thank and so few words to express my gratitude.

To David, my longsuffering husband. You've put up with my various to-ings and fro-ings in life and I appreciate it. Someone once told me it takes a very special person to live with a Machray!

To our children Ruth, Paul, Jonathan & Daniel, sorry for the genes you've inherited and to their spouses, thanks for tolerating them! We appreciate all your support.

To our grandchildren, currently just Beth and Emma, for being such good girls and playing well while Mum, Dad and Gran worked on the editing.

To my editors, Ruth and Fraser, thank you for having the patience of saints whilst untangling what I mean to say from what I've written!

To my son-in-law Andrew, thank you for teaching me to use a computer, I bet you wish you hadn't! We appreciate your work on the website and much more besides.

To our extended family, thank you for all the laughter, the good influences and positive role models which you have been.

To our church family, thank you for your prayers, encouragement and interest in what we were doing.

To our good friends, especially Mairi Galbraith, who have picked us up when we've felt down and inspired some of the aspects of this build, thank you for your input and encouragement.

To Dennis and Muriel, thank you for guiding me through the egg years and encouraging me to take a lead role.

To the Planning to Succeed group & facilitators, those involved in Scottish Enterprise, Visit Scotland especially Chris McCoy, Homelands Trust especially Jan Kerr, the Rambling Roses and a Thorn, and Kenny Mathieson, thank you for keeping telling me I was nearly there and for giving me a better insight into accessibility.

To all those in the Disability Forum who offered planning support when we needed it the most, thank you.

To David Kerridge thank you for the first innovative design, which we loved, you inspired the flexibility for bookings that might be possible.

To our architects, who were prepared to share the financial risk and who got us through planning, bringing the vision through the design phase, thank you for a design worthy of the 2016 Year of Innovation, Architecture and Design.

To Dougie Bissett and his A-Team of builders and suppliers, thank you all for your effort and the quality of your workmanship. You've made the dream a reality. We have a fantastic building which will hopefully be enjoyed by many in years to come.

To those who have provided funding and significant gifts, thank you for your generosity and for embracing the vision.

To the scores of "encouragers" new and old, you have been a voice reminding me that this project is needed and worthwhile. You've kept us going when we stubbed our toes on the stones along the way. Thank you!

To our prospective customers we can't wait for you to come. Thank you for reading this book and thank you for sharing this special journey with us.

Made in the USA
Charleston, SC
08 June 2016